War on the Great Lakes

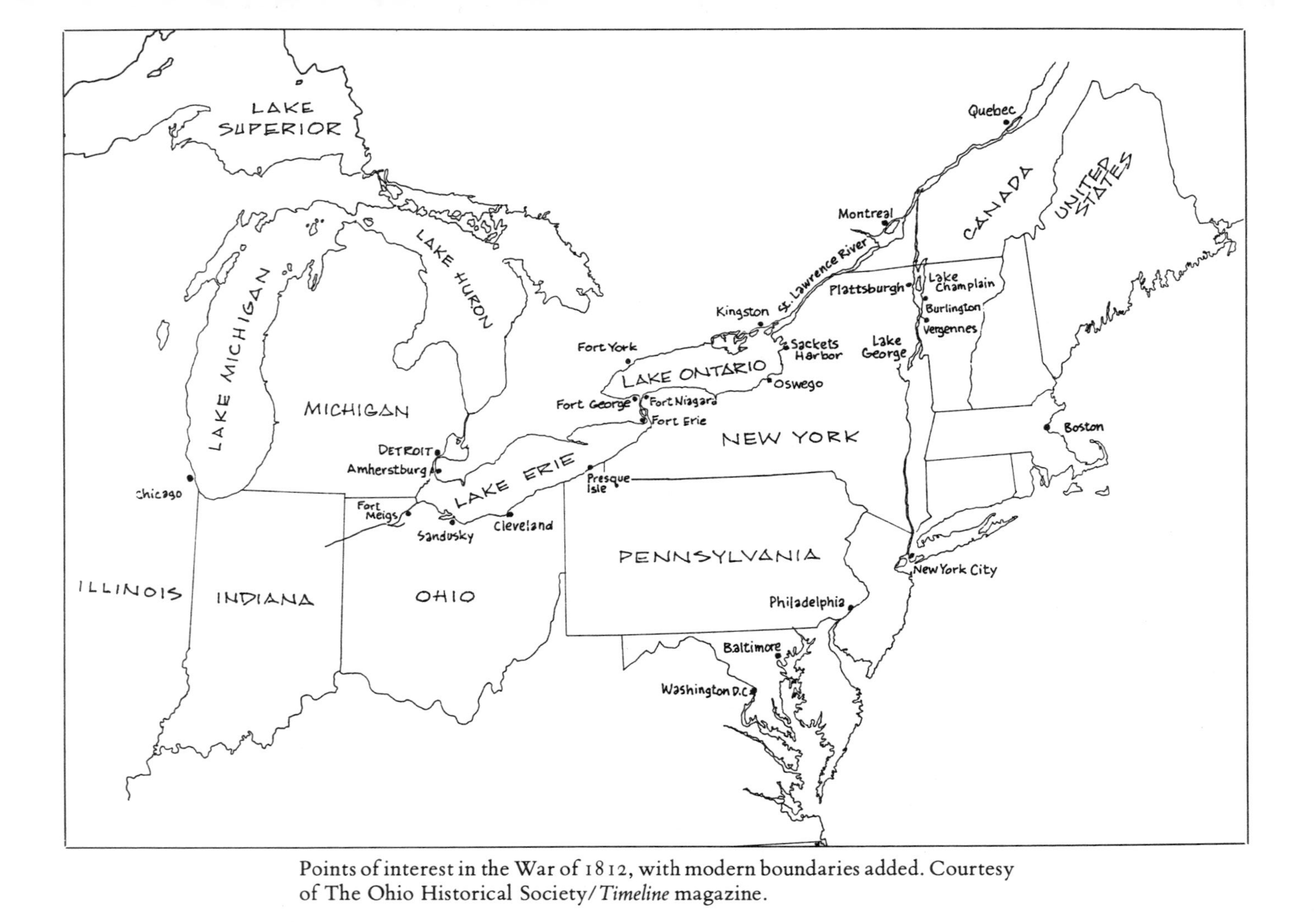

Points of interest in the War of 1812, with modern boundaries added. Courtesy of The Ohio Historical Society/*Timeline* magazine.

War on the Great Lakes

Essays Commemorating the 175th Anniversary of the Battle of Lake Erie

edited by
WILLIAM JEFFREY WELSH
and
DAVID CURTIS SKAGGS

THE KENT STATE UNIVERSITY PRESS
Kent, Ohio, and London, England

Library of Congress Catalog Card Number 90-5345
ISBN 0-87338-424-5 (cloth)
ISBN 0-87338-425-3 (paper)
Manufactured in the United States of America

Library of Congress Cataloging-in-Publication Data

War on the Great Lakes : essays commemorating the 175th anniversary of the Battle of Lake Erie / edited by William Jeffrey Welsh and David Curtis Skaggs.

p. cm.

Papers from the War on the Great Lakes Symposium, held at Windsor, Ont. and Put-in-Bay, Ohio, on Sept. 9–11, 1988.

Includes bibliographical references and index.

ISBN 0-87338-424-5 (cloth : alk. paper) ∞ — ISBN 0-87338-425-3 (pbk. : alk. paper) ∞

1. Erie, Lake, Battle of, 1813—Congresses. I. Welsh, William Jeffrey, 1953- . II. Skaggs, David Curtis. III. War on the Great Lakes Symposium (1988 : Windsor, Ont. and Put-in-Bay, Ohio)

E356.E6W17 1991

973.5'254—dc20 90–5345

British Library Cataloging-in-Publication data are available.

Contents

WILLIAM JEFFREY WELSH
DAVID CURTIS SKAGGS

Introduction

The 175th anniversary of the Battle of Lake Erie spawned a number of scholarly and popular events designed to commemorate the battle and celebrate the century and three-quarters of peace that followed. One such occasion was held at Windsor, Ontario, and Put-in-Bay, Ohio, on September 9–11, 1988. The product of the successful interaction of history professionals from both the United States and Canada, the "War on the Great Lakes Symposium" involved scholars, reenactors, museum personnel, park rangers, teachers, and interested citizens.

One of the most distinguishing features of the celebration was the cruise of the *City of Sandusky,* with 250 participants on board, from Amherstburg, Ontario (the port of the British squadron during the Battle of Lake Erie) to Put-in-Bay, Ohio (the anchorage of the American flotilla). On the site of the engagement that won renown for Master Commandant Oliver Hazard Perry, U.S.N., and which preserved the reputation for valor for Captain Robert Heriot Barclay, R.N., representatives from the Canadian and United States governments tossed wreaths into the water in memory of the brave men who gave their lives 175 years earlier.

Another distinguishing characteristic was the two days of scholarly discussion dedicated to commemorating the Battle of Lake Erie. Whether in the traditional setting of the University of Windsor, on board a lake ferry, or on the steps of Perry's Victory and International Peace Memorial, participants listened to a number of papers dealing with a wide spectrum of topics relating to the War of 1812 and its impact on subsequent relations between the United States and Canada. Ten of those papers are presented herein.

Central to the theme created in this volume is the international perspective of the conference. The planning committee, a consortium of universities and historical sites from both sides of the border, made a conscious effort to overcome any nationalistic prejudices and to provide a truly objective assessment of the war in the Lake Erie basin. While one might find hints of nationalism in the various essays, on the whole the authors are remarkably unbiased in their analyses.

In the opening essay, "The Battle of Lake Erie: A Narrative," Gerard Altoff examines the complex and unusual circumstances which combined to produce an atypical naval struggle on September 10, 1813. According to Altoff, a deficiency of trained seamen, inexperienced officers, and a lack of supplies and materials were factors which made it possible for either belligerent to win the battle.

Another variable which contributed to the outcome of the struggle was the type of guns used during the battle. Frederick Drake's essay, "Artillery and Its Influence on Naval Tactics: Reflections on the Battle of Lake Erie," analyzes the differing broadside capabilities of the two fleets and illustrates how these capabilities determined the tactics adopted by both sides.

Despite the fact that both sides had the ability to win, when the fighting was over, it was Perry's fleet which was victorious. The consequences of the British loss on September 10 is the subject of W. A. B. Douglas's essay, "The Honor of the Flag Had Not Suffered: Robert Heriot Barclay and the Battle of Lake Erie," and Dennis Carter-Edwards's essay, "The Battle of Lake Erie and Its Consequences: Denouement of the British Right Division and Abandonment of the Western District to American Troops, 1813–1815." Douglas grapples with the contradictory reactions to Barclay's defeat. He points out that while merchants who traded in Canada showered Barclay with gifts, the Admiralty ignored him for more than ten years after the battle. Douglas reevaluates these responses by considering the battle from Barclay's point of view.

Meanwhile, Carter-Edwards examines the aftermath of Barclay's defeat by placing it in the larger context of its impact on the British war effort. He argues that despite the loss of the Western District, the British successfully defended the colony. The loss had no significant impact on the war effort. Rather, the effects were local. The careers of Barclay and Procter suffered, the local residents of the Western District fell under the jurisdiction of the United States, and the native people who fought with the British were abandoned by their former allies.

David Edmunds, in his essay, "Tecumseh's Native Allies: Warriors Who Fought for the Crown," analyzes in further detail the issue of Indian allies of the British. Following a brief survey of the conditions amongst the tribes in the Old Northwest during the decade preceding the War of 1812, he discusses those factors which encouraged most Indians to side with the Crown. In particular, he outlines the lives of Tecumseh's allied chiefs and their long-forgotten careers.

While many of the essays explore military aspects of the battle, Harold Langley's contribution, "The Quest for Peace in the War of 1812," describes the diplomatic events which occurred after the battle and which resulted in the signing of the Treaty of Ghent on December 24, 1814. Delivered at Put-in-Bay on the 175th anniversary of the Battle of Lake Erie, Langley's essay capstoned a symposium dedicated to commemorating the international peace that followed the War of 1812.

The symposium also sought to provide a look at the possibilities of new research opportunities. Ian Pemberton's often humorous examination of Canadian historiography of the war and Christopher McKee's "aerial" survey of United States historiography point out not only what has been explored but also what new opportunities still exist as we enter the last years of the second century since the battle. No one who wishes to engage in such an enterprise will want to begin without first consulting Stuart Sutherland's guide to Canadian archives and Doug Clanin's exhaustive bibliography of United States manuscript sources—a treasure trove worthy of close examination and use.

On a more personal note, we, like editors before us, were not spared the task of having to select the correct spelling of a proper name from a myriad of choices. A case in point is that of Henry Procter. Many works, including J. C. A. Stagg's *Mr. Madison's War,* have chosen the Proctor spelling. We chose the "er" spelling because his official correspondence was signed that way in the fall of 1813.

Determining Procter's rank, during the summer and fall of 1813, was also troublesome. In August, he signed his correspondence Lt. Colonel; in September, it was Major-General.[1] Therefore, during the battle, Procter is referred to as Major-General. During the period prior to the battle, he is referred to as Lt. Colonel.

One final issue was the spelling of Sacket's Harbor. Despite the efforts of nineteenth-century cartographers to change it to Sacketts Harbor, the land belonged to Augustus Sacket and we have decided that the correct spelling is Sacket's Harbor.

In closing, the editors of this volume would like to thank the over five hundred participants in the symposium, cruise, parade, and encampment that were part of the 175th anniversary celebration for making this event a memorable, instructional, and lasting experience. Particular attention should be paid to those agencies which provided financial assistance, personnel time, and expertise: Bowling Green State University; Environment Canada—Canadian Parks Service; Daughters of the War of 1812; Essex County (Ontario) Historical Society; Firelands College—Lake Erie Regional Studies Program; Fort Malden National Historic Park; Fort Meigs State Memorial; Hiram Walker Historical Museum; Maumee Valley Historical Society; Monroe County (Michigan) Historical Museum; Ohio Historical Society; Ohio Humanities Council; Ontario Ministry of Culture and Communications; Perry's Victory and International Peace Memorial; United States National Park Service; University of Windsor; Convention and Visitors Bureaus of Windsor, Essex County, and Pelee Island; and the Chambers of Commerce of Amherstburg, Anderdon, and Malden.

Finally, we would like to thank the members of the planning committee, of which we were a part: Gerry Altoff, Dennis Au, Harry Bosveld, Alan Douglas, Harry Myers, Larry Nelson, Ian Pemberton, John Steinle, David Webb. For their exertions, Mother Nature provided an absolutely beautiful late summer weekend on which was commemorated an important naval engagement and the even more significant advent of peace on the Great Lakes.

William Jeffrey Welsh
Lake Erie Regional Studies Program
Firelands College

David Curtis Skaggs
Department of History
Bowling Green State University

GERARD T. ALTOFF

The Battle of Lake Erie: A Narrative

Blood streamed in crimson rivulets along the seams of the stricken ship's gouged deck. As their lifeblood flowed from ghastly wounds, tortured seamen writhed in agony, their heart-rending screams and moans competing with the roar of cannon and musketry. The broken and maimed bodies lying on deck or stretched out in the surgery below far outnumbered the exhausted and mentally stunned sailors still on their feet. Thick clouds of dirty white gunsmoke drifted across the restless lake, its rancid, sulfurous smell pervading every corner of the ravaged vessel, stinging the eyes and wrinkling the nostrils of the ship's dazed crew. Like walking zombies they stumbled about their assigned duties, brains refusing to register the horror surrounding them.

The little 20-gun brig, battered and beaten, shuddered under the impact of each British cannonball, as if in sympathy for the wretched men bleeding on her deck. Her gunports were mostly silent, only a few of the giant 32-pounders still capable of disgorging their deadly iron spheres. Shredded strips of canvas flapped helplessly in the wind, all that remained of the ship's once majestic sails. Rigging hung limply from her spars and trailed in the water alongside, not unlike a stately willow after a hailstorm. Her tall, heavily punctured frame resembled a bull's-eye after a long day of target practice.

On the flayed quarterdeck the young commodore, hatless and wearing a common seaman's round-jacket to conceal him from British sharpshooters, gazed despairingly at the wasted wreck that only two hours earlier had been the proud flagship of his fleet. Peering up at the large blue banner floating above his head on the main truck—his battle flag bearing the determined epithet "DONT GIVE UP THE SHIP"—he perceived that its taunting words belied his desperate situation. Surrender appeared his only logical alternative.

It was an incredible predicament for an officer who exactly one month earlier had resigned his commission from the U.S. Navy. Master Commandant Oliver Hazard Perry had undoubtedly suffered a number of both real and imagined slights from his superior, Commodore Isaac Chauncey, during the summer of 1813. Not least of these affronts was Chauncey's railing vilification after Perry bypassed his commanding officer and appealed directly to Secretary of the Navy William Jones for assistance, an obvious error in judgment by Perry.

Throughout the previous spring Chauncey had supported Perry while the American fleet was under construction at Erie, Pennsylvania, and the latter was able to solve most of his shipbuilding problems through diligence and hard work. However, as the time neared to fight his fleet, Perry was forced to rely on Chauncey to provide sailors, but progress to resolve his manpower shortage was nil. All reinforcements for the Great Lakes were routed through Sacket's Harbor, New York, for distribution by Chauncey who churlishly, though perhaps understandably, elected to retain the cream of the crop for his own Lake Ontario fleet. Even after Chauncey relented, thanks to Perry's missive and Jones's intervention, and provided two contingents of sailors for the Erie fleet, Perry still fell far short of his manpower requirements. Needing a minimum of 720 able-bodied seamen to man his numerous vessels, Perry could muster only about 400 men by August 10. Of this number fully one-fourth were soldier volunteers or marines, and a large number were prostrated by a debilitating lake-induced fever, a malady with which Perry himself was intermittently afflicted.

Chauncey's apparent disregard for both Perry's military situation and personal feelings compelled Perry to submit his resignation to Secretary Jones. While deadly serious, Perry was nevertheless cognizant of his greater responsibilities, those being duty to his country and Major-General William Henry Harrison's critical situation in northwest Ohio. Several weeks would pass before a suitable replacement could reach Lake Erie. Meanwhile, Perry would strive to accomplish his assigned task, the destruction of British naval power on Lake Erie.

Realizing that further reinforcements from Sacket's Harbor would not be forthcoming, Perry decided to sail for western Lake Erie. Although hindered by his lack of seamen, Perry was determined this handicap would not inhibit him. On August 12, with barely enough men to navigate his ships, Perry aimed his bowsprits toward the setting sun.

Even though at this point he commanded too few men to even fill his gun crews, Perry was confident his dilemma would somehow be rectified. He had labored too long and hard to be deprived of the opportunity to fight his fleet.

The American fleet, ten vessels strong, arrived off Sandusky Bay on August 16. Harrison, Perry, and their combined staffs held a conference on board the flagship *Lawrence* to determine strategy. Here it was decided that Perry would utilize Put-in-Bay harbor on South Bass Island as his base of operations. From that strategic location Perry could easily observe British fleet movements in the event they opted to sail, or interdict enemy supply vessels if they attempted a hasty resupply mission.

Twice in the next three weeks, sailing from his new base, Perry conducted reconnaissance cruises in the proximity of Fort Malden. Perry hoped a direct approach and bombardment of both the fort and the Amherstburg Navy Yard might prove the simplest and easiest means of destroying the British. Such was not the case. The fort was too strongly defended, the current in the Detroit River too swift, the winds too fickle, and the channel too narrow for fleet maneuvers. In any event, it was not necesssary for Perry to risk his fleet in an ill-conceived attack; time was now on the American side.

With the American fleet perched in western Lake Erie the British confronted numerical superiority. More importantly, their water supply route along Lake Erie's northern shore between Fort Malden and Long Point was compromised. Perry need only return to Put-in-Bay, train his hybrid crews of soldiers and sailors, and wait for the British to sail forth and fight.

Perry's adversary, Robert Heriot Barclay, was younger than Perry by a year, yet he was an experienced Royal Navy officer who had lost an arm fighting against the French in the Napoleonic Wars. There was little doubt in Barclay's mind that a battle was forthcoming, and even less doubt that he would wage the fight at a considerable disadvantage. Despite the fact that Barclay commanded fewer ships than Perry, he nevertheless counted more cannon lining his broadsides—nine American ships with fifty-four guns versus six British vessels with sixty-three artillery pieces. But it was not the number of muzzles that really mattered. What would determine the outcome of the upcoming battle was the weight of metal those broadsides fired. The American ships were armed primarily with heavy 32-pounders, while Barclay's largest guns were 24-pounders, and he was equipped with all too few of those. Barclay's meager hopes lay in the fact that most of his guns were long-range weapons.

Perry relied on carronades for his two largest ships. Although they were endowed with numerous practical advantages over the traditional naval cannon, carronades possessed less than half the effective range of the British long guns. Essentially, the Americans traded firepower for distance. Thus, if Barclay could maintain his fleet at long range, he could pulverize the American vessels before Perry's short-range guns inflicted fatal damage.

Guns, however, were not Barclay's only worry. As destitute as Perry was of trained sailors, Barclay found himself even more shorthanded. The British commodore on Lake Ontario and Barclay's immediate superior, Sir James Lucas Yeo, proved even more parsimonious with resources than Chauncey. When Barclay arrived at Amherstburg, his largest vessel could boast only twenty experienced seamen, a situation that did not greatly improve. As a result, crews on the English ships were comprised mostly of British soldiers, Canadian militia, and merchant mariners. Barclay surely contemplated the upcoming engagement with nervous uncertainty.

Significant though these deficiencies were, it was an entirely different factor that forced Barclay's hand. With the British supply line severed by Perry's presence at Put-in-Bay, the store of rations at Fort Malden was soon depleted. By September 9, only one day's supply of flour remained, so there was really no option. The British could either regain control of Lake Erie and their interrupted supply line, or abandon Fort Malden, their Indian allies, and the fruits of their earlier hard-won victories.

Whereas Barclay could expect no additional help, Perry received welcome reinforcements upon returning to Put-in-Bay from his Fort Malden sojourn. After discovering Perry's paucity of seamen during their initial meeting two weeks earlier, Harrison issued a call for volunteers from among his regiments. Altogether approximately 130 men volunteered, soldiers from all the regular regiments in the Old Northwest plus a number of militia units. Of Perry's eventual total of 532 men on his ten vessels, over 40 percent were assimilated soldiers and marines emanating from nearly twenty different army units representing at least ten different states; an incredible amalgamation of diverse elements never before nor since assembled to fight a fleet of American warships.

The stage was set. Barclay consulted with Major-General Henry Procter, commander of combined British operations in the Old Northwest, and it was decided Barclay would fight the American fleet. Regardless of his problems and shortages, no choice remained for

Barclay except a fleet action at a time and place not of his choosing. On the afternoon of September 9, 1813, the British ships hauled their hooks, floated down the Detroit River, and slipped into Lake Erie.

As a crisp dawn slowly crept across the placid waters and peaceful islands, a lookout perched at dizzying heights above the deck of the American flagship suddenly bellowed a warning. Perry, in his cabin below, rushed on deck barking commands. Scurrying about in disciplined chaos, barefoot sailors responded to their lieutenants' shouted orders and hurriedly executed a myriad of complex evolutions. As the stars and stripes lazily floated from the main gaffs, the long line of nine vessels eased out of Put-in-Bay—the schooner *Ohio* having been dispatched a few days earlier for supplies.

Perry's first concern after clearing the harbor was to position his fleet to windward of the British so as to acquire the crucial advantage of the weather gauge. A small forest of British masts stood starkly visible several miles north of Rattlesnake Island. A gentle breeze, barely strong enough to ruffle the calm waters, puffed intermittently from the southwest. To secure the weather gauge Perry would find it necessary to work his vessels well to the westward of Rattlesnake Island, but the southwesterly breeze was blowing almost directly in his face, obviating any opportunity of headreaching to windward. If the British continued to hold the wind advantage, they could maintain a sufficient distance to windward and destroy Perry's fleet with their long guns before the American commodore managed to deploy his short-range carronades. Perry's small schooners did carry heavy long guns, but only one or two each, certainly not enough to deflect the British onslaught. With the leverage of the weather gauge the British could focus on one American vessel at a time and destroy Perry's fleet piecemeal.

For almost three hours Perry's heels rapped a steady tattoo as he impatiently paced back and forth across the *Lawrence*'s quarterdeck, interrupted only occasionally by a frustrated scowl in the direction of the British ships. No matter how arrantly he willed it, Perry's ships failed to make headway into the wind. Finally, at four bells in the forenoon watch (ten o'clock A.M.), a disgusted Perry succumbed to nature's vagary and passed the order to wear ship and steer an easterly course. Conceding the salient advantage of the weather gauge to the British, Perry now intended to fight to leeward among the islands, where Barclay's superiority of long guns might conceivably eliminate American naval power on Lake Erie. Perry's action illustrates his overpowering desire to fight and prove his squadron, but it also points to a certain rashness and impetuosity in his personality.

Fortunately the consequences of Perry's headstrong decision will never be known. No sooner was this inexpedient order issued than the mutable wind suddenly backed ninety degrees and blew from the southeast. An incredible stroke of good fortune, the change of wind direction, as Barclay later recounted, proffered a prodigious advantage to the American fleet. Mother Nature had conferred upon Perry the one factor over which he had no control: a wind at his back.

The sinking feeling in Barclay's chest served only to emphasize a rapidly deteriorating state of affairs. Barclay had just lost his one great advantage but he was not about to submit. With a little ingenuity and a modicum of good fortune the battle could still be won. Although the breeze favored the Americans, it was barely strong enough to propel a ship through the water. Perry's approach would thus be exceedingly prolonged, and a slow approach would allow time for Barclay's more numerous long guns to play upon the American ships virtually unchallenged. If Barclay could dismast or disable one or both of the American brigs before Perry's deadly carronades floated into range the day could yet belong to the British.

Barclay's iota of optimism increased as he stared intently at the still distant American line. Ever so slowly the American fleet appeared to be splitting apart. The smaller converted merchant vessels bringing up the rear of Perry's line were deep-hulled vessels designed to carry cargo, not cannon. Unfortunately the combination of deep draft and impotent winds soon forced three schooners and a sloop to lag behind, isolating half of Perry's heavy long guns far astern and temporarily out of the battle. Even though these four small vessels carried only one or two long guns each, all were 32- or 24-pounders, a heavy punch indeed. Barclay's fortunes were steadily improving.

Perry elected not to wait for his wayward schooners, once again exhibiting a lack of constraint and displaying possibly faulty judgment. There was obviously no hurry since the British had no option but to fight, they were going nowhere. Perry must have realized that, yet he deliberately dashed pell-mell into range of the enemy long guns, leaving many of his own heavy long guns trailing in his wake, guns that could equally contest the British and somewhat negate the enemy advantage.

The light airs instead insured that Perry, in such a great hurry, would make only faltering progress. The two fleets converged with painful slowness. Perry opted to use this pregnant interval to display his as-yet-unseen battleflag. Sewn by a dowager acquaintance of Perry's in Erie, the banner was a blue rectangle sporting crude white letters. The message on the flag, though negative in connotation, left no doubt as to its meaning. It was the dying utterance of Perry's friend, the epitaph of the man for whom his flagship was named—James Lawrence. As the navy blue bunting fluttered to the maintruck and its words were read by upraised eyes, the phrase "DONT GIVE UP THE SHIP" inspired a chorus of throaty, boisterous cheers—tension-relieving cheers, just as Perry intended. But as the dying echoes of the spirited shouting dissipated over the open water, the trepidation again began to mount. Nothing now remained except the intolerable waiting and last minute preparations.

Reticence gripped the crewmen as they nervously pondered the coming few hours. Hearts thumped irregularly, muscles knotted in tensed shoulders, eyes squinted against the shimmering glare, dry tongues licked parched lips, sweaty palms stroked cotton trousers, stiffened fingers clenched and unclenched, restless feet shuffled against white holystoned decks. Only a few nervous coughs punctuated the silence.

The clean decks were sanded to help retain footing on the inevitably blood-splattered, smooth wood. Buckets of water dotted the planking, to quell both thirst and the nemesis of all sailors—fire. Ramrods clinked as soldiers and marines jammed musketballs down long-barreled smoothbores. Slow-match burned in sand-filled tubs. Gun captains minutely inspected the bulbous cannonballs, searching for imperfections that would prevent the iron spheres from flying true. Gun crews triple-checked rammers, sponges, thumbstalls, tackleblocks, and flaked gun-tackle; inexperienced officers paced anxiously; marines with fixed bayonets guarded the hatches, ordered to cut down cowards attempting to skulk below. In the sick bays, surgeons in leather aprons laid out orderly rows of scalpels, probes, lancets, and bone saws, while their hated loblolly boys waited patiently, unemotionally to restrain the bloodied, mangled wounded; powder monkeys scampered to and fro with deadly fodder for the insatiable big guns; agitated and frightened men craned flushed faces above bulwarks, swearing the opposing fleets were drawing no closer. But they were!

At 11:45 A.M. the unearthly silence was broken when a brilliant flash highlighted the steep profile of Barclay's flagship and a thunderous crash echoed across the tranquil water. A ranging shot which splashed harmlessly short of the *Lawrence.* The waiting was over.

The encore was not long in coming as the British soon opened a steady fire. Ten minutes after the opening volley Perry hoisted a signal for all vessels to close the range and engage their previously designated adversaries. Obviously that was impossible for the lagging schooners, yet Perry was not overly concerned. *Lawrence* was moving slowly but steadily and *Niagara* coasted under all sail only a quarter mile astern. The brigs *Lawrence* and *Niagara* carried forty of Perry's fifty-four guns, thirty-six of which were the heavy 32-pounder carronades. As long as *Lawrence,* Perry's flagship, closed with *Detroit,* Barclay's flagship, and *Niagara* converged with *Queen Charlotte,* Barclay's second largest ship, then Perry would maintain better than a three-to-two advantage in weight of broadsides. If only he could absorb the punishment until the range shortened, Perry knew Barclay was finished.

For thirty minutes British metal crashed into the *Lawrence* and American soldiers and sailors died horribly or were smashed screaming to her deck. Retribution was impossible; the range was too great. The Americans could only grit their teeth, brave the storm of shot, and pray for a stronger breeze.

Finally, at 12:15 P.M., the *Lawrence* eased into range. Perry luffed and his ponderous 32-pounders belched iron death at the British. His ship had been hurt, but not mortally, and all her guns were in action. All Perry needed now was the *Niagara.* With an additional broadside of 32-pounder carronades, the pendulum would inevitably swing to the American side, and the British would find themselves inundated by American metal.

But as Perry glanced astern he was unsure his eyes were focusing properly. Through the dense gunsmoke it appeared *Niagara* had brailed her jib and backed her main topsail. It was a nightmare. *Niagara* had indeed shortened sail and stalled her forward progress, leaving the unbelieving crew of the *Lawrence* aghast and bewildered.

The actions of *Niagara*'s commander, Jesse Elliott, were unclear at the time and have been further obfuscated over the passing years. In the long run his motives are irrelevant. What mattered was the *Niagara* failed to close *Queen Charlotte* and that by his actions Elliott doomed the *Lawrence* and her beleaguered crew.

With no opponent for her own carronades *Queen Charlotte* swung out of line and pulled forward, leveling her broadside at the *Lawrence.* Following her lead was *General Hunter,* also blazing away at the *Lawrence.* With *Niagara* timorously shying away and Perry's smaller supporting vessels virtually ignored, the British pinpointed the combined broadsides of their three largest vessels on Perry's isolated flagship. For two endless hours *Lawrence*'s crewmen suffered systematic and excruciating torment while Elliott, aboard *Niagara,* wallowed ineffectually out of range, little more than a spectator.

Shortly after *Queen Charlotte* gathered way and pushed ahead in the

British line, *Niagara* again set sail and glided forward. Inexplicably, however, Elliott hugged the wind, sliding away from the British line. His later recollections indicated he was attempting to assault the head of the British line, a redundant goal he was unable to achieve even after a two-hour time span. Elliott was conscious of the terrible destruction suffered by the American flagship, but he made no concerted effort to close with the enemy line as per Perry's specific order.[1]

By 2:30 P.M. the plight of the ravaged *Lawrence* almost defied description. At best she was a defenseless hulk. Pride welled up in Perry's chest at the superb performance and superhuman sacrifice manifested by his incomparable crew, a sacrifice he could not mock by ignominious surrender.

Staring at the proud words emblazoned on his battle standard, still straining against its halyard at the main top, Perry realized he had no choice but to betray its unyielding tenor and abandon his precious ship. Anguished by his decision and feeling the questioning stares of the many wounded and the few sailors still on their feet, Perry ordered the damaged, but usable, small boat prepared and his battle flag hauled down.

Moments earlier Perry had glimpsed the *Niagara* approximately one-half mile to windward, her unseeming serenity a haunting visage compared to the horror of *Lawrence*'s gundeck. Anger and frustration sparked the image of a plan. Rounding up four unwounded seamen—no easy task—Perry manned the amazingly intact cutter and pulled for *Niagara.* Straining at the oars the already exhausted sailors were spurred on by the incessant splash of British shot.

It was a simple matter for the British to recognize Perry's strategy. Only a few minutes before, the promise of victory leaned toward the Union Jack; however, if Perry was allowed to engage a fresh battery the day might yet be lost. Every effort was put forth to smother the tiny rowboat skimming over the waves. Again and again sweating British gunners rammed powder, wad, cannonball, another wad, finally touching off the shot they hoped would win the battle. Deafened and dazed by the constant roar and bone-jarring concussion of thunderous cannonading, their actions were nevertheless swift and automatic, the product of training, discipline, and proud British naval tradition.

The little skiff disappeared in the splash of British cannonballs, only to reappear unscathed, its oarsmen and daring commodore soaked to the skin but otherwise unharmed. Again it disappeared, and still again, each time miraculously sculling clear from the storm of shot and funnels of falling water. Finally, after a harrowing and terrifying journey of about fifteen minutes, the frail cutter and its soggy occupants gratefully slipped under the protective sheer of the looming *Niagara.*

The dialogue which ensued after Perry boarded *Niagara* can only be imagined; accounts vary depending on the eyewitness reporter. Regardless of what was said, however, Elliott apparently volunteered to relinquish command of his own undamaged vessel, depart his ship in Perry's small boat, and row back to hurry along the lagging schooners.

Perry, not surprisingly, exerted no effort to defer or delay Elliott's departure. After conducting a brief survey to determine *Niagara*'s fighting capabilities Perry rapped out a string of orders. Sailors scampered up *Niagara*'s ratlines and scurried along the footropes of her giant yards, shaking out the reefed canvas, which instantly bellied out in the freshening wind. The menacing mouths of her cold carronades were each stuffed with two heavy six-inch cannonballs. Soldiers in the fighting tops anxiously fingered the hammers of their muskets. At last the *Niagara*'s earnest and willing crew were about to join the fray.

Eyes widened in shock as British officers and seamen viewed the truculent apparition approaching through the dissolving gunsmoke. After two hours of blood and suffering, they had defeated the American flagship; by rights they should have won the day. The unimpaired brig now running down on their line was like a slap in the face.

Although completely wrecked, the *Lawrence* had nevertheless succeeded in meting out harsh punishment to her opponents. British casualties had been severe. Barclay himself was wounded early in the battle, but he endured the pain and managed to stay the deck. Then, as *Niagara* neared the British line Barclay suffered a second wound, this one serious enough to force him below to the surgeon. In fact, by the time *Niagara* bore down on the British line the captain and first officer of every British ship had been either killed or wounded. Inexperienced junior officers now commanded these complex vessels of war. Certainly they were brave men, but they were uninitiated and untutored in directing complex fighting vessels in a complicated naval engagement.

The British were all too aware that only one tactic might preserve them from *Niagara*'s fresh broadsides. If they could manage to wear ship—turn the vessels 180 degrees—then the guns on their starboard sides, not yet engaged, could be brought to bear. Far too many of their larboard guns had been disabled; a successful repulse of the enemy was entirely dependent on those unused starboard broadsides.

Haste was imperative, *Niagara* was rapidly bearing down on the British line. Orders were prescribed and British sailors strained at the braces. The ravaged British flagship slowly turned with the wind—all too slowly. Having borne the brunt of *Lawrence*'s guns, *Detroit*'s sails, spars, and rigging were heavily damaged. Mistiming the evolution, the confused junior officer commanding the *Queen Charlotte* failed to judge *Detroit*'s sluggish movements and pressed on too much canvas. Before any remedial action could be initiated, *Queen Charlotte*'s bowsprit plunged squarely into *Detroit*'s mizzen rigging, creating a tangled mess that would require precious minutes to hack away, minutes that would cost the British dearly. Now, at the most critical phase of the battle, the two largest British ships were locked together and helpless.

Perry thrust the *Niagara* mid-point between the British battle line—three "sail" to starboard, three to larboard. Twenty gun captains jerked twenty lanyards and *Niagara* was instantly shrouded in acrid smoke. A mind-numbing blast rippled the dispassionate water as forty heavy cannonballs sped on their destructive mission. Sponge, load, fire! Sponge, load, fire!

Dozens of jagged holes abruptly disfigured the flanks of Barclay's ships. Masts quivered like trees feeling the axe; loud tearing noises presaged the shredding of blossoming canvas; hundreds of deadly wood splinters purged the disarrayed decks; British and Canadian blood flowed freely.

After turbulent minutes of hacking and slashing, with many of those wielding the axes cut down in the process, *Detroit* and *Queen Charlotte* cleared the discordant clutter of entangled rigging and eased apart. But by then it was too late. Too few guns were capable of firing, too few gunners remained standing. Other than death and total destruction only one option was left. *Detroit,* her imposing ensign prominently nailed to the mast, fired a gun off her disengaged side, signaling her surrender. Moments later a white flag slowly ascended from *Queen Charlotte*'s deck, while *General Hunter* and *Lady Prevost* similarly signified their surrender. The two smallest British vessels, *Chippewa* and *Little Belt,* shook out their sails to make a run for it, closely pursued by two American ships. It proved a short chase. A shot across their bows impressed upon the British the futility of flight and the last two enemy vessels soon capitulated. The entire British fleet had been captured.

At first the silence, after three hours of earsplitting pandemonium, was perplexing; but after a few minutes Perry began to grasp the enormity of his success. His victory proved to be the first time in all of British naval history that an entire fleet of warships had been captured. Harrison must be informed! Finding an old letter Perry hastily scribbled on the back of the envelope,

> Dear General:
> We have met the enemy and they are ours. Two ships, two brigs, one schooner, and a sloop.
> Yours with great respect and esteem,
>
> O. H. Perry

At long last Lake Erie was in American hands. William Henry Harrison now possessed the crucial component necessary to transport men and supplies rapidly and simply across the lake, the precise factor required to launch his long delayed invasion. Oliver Hazard Perry achieved what he set out to do, and in the process immortalized himself in American naval lore.[2]

FREDERICK C. DRAKE

Artillery and Its Influence on Naval Tactics: Reflections on the Battle of Lake Erie

> For it is obvious that a fleet possessing, say, a superiority of heavy-shotted but short-ranged guns will seek to fight an action in a way entirely different from that chosen by a fleet which has as its strong suit, the light-shotted, long-range gun. Tactics are—and must be—dictated by both these considerations, and not by one or the other of them alone.
>
> —Michael Lewis, "Armada Guns"

The idea for this paper developed out of a presentation made at Kingston to the joint meeting of the Canadian Nautical Research Society and the North American Society for Nautical Research on May 22, 1987. A modified version of that paper was later presented at the Eighth Naval History Symposium at Annapolis, Maryland, as "Commodore Sir James Lucas Yeo and Governor General Sir George Prevost: A Study in Command Relations, 1813–1814."[1] That paper ended with a comparison of Commodore Isaac Chauncey's[2] and James Lucas Yeo's[3] available guns and the composition of their squadrons, how those guns and battery strengths were perceived, and how each commander would not, indeed could not, engage unless on terms when the particular strengths of his guns would reinforce his perception of the sailing advantage possessed by his squadron. Hence, except running skirmishes, there was no battle.

In a postconference analysis in the officer's club at Annapolis, David Skaggs asked if a similar study of artillery and its influence on naval tactics for Lake Erie was possible. That is difficult for three reasons. While Yeo and Chauncey spent the war in a studied pursuit of each other to gain maximum advantage at various times with minimum damage, Robert Heriot Barclay and Oliver Hazard Perry in the end, as we all know, engaged in the ding-dong battle that Barclay hoped would break Perry's blockade of his squadron at the western end of the lake, and which Perry hoped would secure it permanently. In other words, the context of naval action produced tactical results spectacularly different from the Ontario scene. Second, the personalities of Perry and Barclay were quite different from those of Chauncey and Yeo, and the personality of the commanders was often of more importance than the guns they carried on board the ships they sailed. Third, "It is all really a question of degree," as Michael Lewis pointed out almost fifty years ago in his seminal classification of the Armada guns, "—of degree, that is, in each category of alleged superiority: leadership, seamanship, ships, and guns,"[4] when a historian studies any naval action. In other words, any study that focuses *just* on guns—naval artillery—and leaves out other factors—Michael Lewis's "factors of degree," or "questions of emphasis," as he termed it elsewhere—would be in grave danger of appearing to concentrate on single factor analysis.

A further factor to be considered is the type of guns that were in use upon the war vessels in 1812. Two ships might be of the same number of guns and be the same size but still be of very unequal force. William James gives an example of a 12-pounder frigate and an 18-pounder frigate in which the latter is nearly double the total battery power of the former.[5] The type of guns, then, can make a great difference in a contest. The two main types in 1812 were varieties of long guns and carronades. The former were much longer and thicker barreled than the latter, and the size varied from 2- to 42-pounders. The carronades were much lighter, had a larger bore, and threw a heavier ball, as compared to a long gun of the same weight, but for a much shorter distance. Should a vessel carrying long guns meet one with carronades, unless the latter could close to short range quickly, she was likely to be overmatched at distance, even if everything else was equal.

Other factors intrude naturally. On Ontario in 1813, for example, the duel between Yeo and Chauncey was circumscribed by shipbuilding, raiding lake bases, skirmishing with each other, cooperating with their compatriot army commanders in combined operations, undertaking logistical work supplying the armies in the Niagara peninsula, and blockading each other's squadrons at various times. In those circumstances the overriding strategical consideration for Yeo was that he had to fight a holding action in order to reinforce the army's ability to hold the territory; and Chauncey had to win the initiative, not only tactically, on the lake, but strategically by removing the impediment of his opponent's squadron to facilitate invasion of the territory. On Ontario, thus, the composition of the squadrons, as well as the respective perceptions and attitudes of the commanders, made it unlikely that either commander would wish to risk his vessels in conditions regarded as most favorable for his opponent.[6] On Erie, Perry, like Chauncey for Ontario, faced a similar problem of removing the impediment of his opponent's squadron. Yet his squadron predominated in carronades like Yeo's, while Barclay's was more balanced, like Chauncey's. Yet tactically and strategically, Barclay was on the defensive in relation to Perry. Simply put, Barclay had a balance *vis-à-vis* his opponent, like Chauncey in relation to Yeo, but his strategical and tactical position was like Yeo's in relation to Chauncey. Therefore, why did Barclay fight in September 1813, and how did artillery influence the tactics when he did? One of the suggestions of this paper is that perhaps Barclay should not have fought at all, or, perhaps, not fought the kind of action he chose on September 10.

Guns and personalities often produce strange mixes. Generally, as Lewis indicated, in any action guns should be looked at as either battery (ship-killers) or as rapid-fire (man-killers).[7] How they are apportioned on board different vessels affects the tactics of battle. In battle, different opportunities may be presented for different guns. Different charges of powder for different weights of single shot, double shot, or chain shot produce different results and demand different targets. Even though broadside-to-broadside is the orthodox way of describing actions, as can be seen in accounts of this war ranging from James to Cooper, Roosevelt to Mahan, the weight of shot fired in batteries should not only be compared with the weight of shot fired by the opponent, but, if possible, should be mentioned with the *defensive* power of the ship receiving that shot. James Fenimore Cooper articulated this problem in the introduction to his naval history of the United States.[8] Moreover, the range of guns should be calculated also, for some guns perform to a maximum capacity at distances farther from their target than do other guns. Guns are thus merely one of a number of factors involved in the process of reaching a decision in any battle, and how their commanders choose to use them is often of critical importance.

Nevertheless, most writers still tend to determine the comparative value of ship actions by comparing the weight of metal thrown in any one broadside.[9] This method was taken to the extreme by Theodore Roosevelt, who compared the ratios of people killed between two vessels with the rate of the weight of metal thrown, and concluded, in most cases, that vastly superior gunnery was evident upon the side of the Americans. This assumption is open to criticism generally and in the case of Lake Erie in particular, and later writers on the war have steered sharply away from it.[10] Other factors, however, influence the results of an action. In some actions in the war, the accounts indicate that the guns were "double shotted," or "treble shotted," or with the broadsides filled alternately with round shot, then grape shot, or canister shot, thus switching from ship-killing to man-killing alternately. Yet again, alternate guns have bags of musquet balls wedged home to be fired. Taking the weight of metal in broadside fired as the number of guns in broadside multiplied by the weight of *one* shot thrown can be misleading as to the actual extent of the broadside fired or the action engaged. Man-killing or sail- and rigging-shredding may predominate at key times in an action.

On Erie, the contest for the British was becoming critical in late summer 1813. The British superiority between May and August was slowly being eroded.[11] Barclay had come to a small Canadian provincial marine squadron, the largest vessel of which was the *Queen Charlotte,* a ship then carrying ten 24-pounder carronades and six long guns, a boatswain, a carpenter, and twenty-five crew.[12] His task was to preserve a superiority of force on the lake in face of the rising threat to it, as his opponent was efficiently building both ships and a naval establishment at Erie.

Barclay and Perry were not only efficient, but both were interested in having heavy guns (ship-killers) rather than light ones on board. While Barclay had commanded at Kingston, he had suggested to Sir George Prevost, British commander-in-chief in the Canadas, the laying down of at least ten gun boats to carry one 18- or 24-pounder in the bow, and a carronade in the stern, and had later ordered six to be built. At the same time he ordered thirty large guns to be forwarded to Kingston: six 42-pounders, twelve 24s, and twelve 18s.[13] He lost the guns intended for the Erie establishment when Chauncey and General Dearborn raided York in April 1813, and destroyed twenty-eight cannons ranging from 6- to 32-pounders together with a large amount of stores intended to be forwarded to Amherstburg.[14] When Barclay arrived at Amherstburg, he set to work exercising his men twice a day at what guns were available for periods of one and a half to two hours each time. Perry, likewise, seemed to prefer the heavy 32-pounder carronades that Chauncey arranged to have shipped to his naval establishment at Presque Isle; and he may have had more than the sixty-five guns on station that Rosenberg credits him with, for he made efforts to add to them from Black Rock. For example, in addition to the guns forwarded from Washington, Sacket's Harbor, and New York, his letterbook reveals on

May 7, 1813, that he received a 32-pounder up from Buffalo and sent three boats down the moment the weather was suitable for the others. On May 9, he ordered Lieutenant Thomas Holdup to bring two more with slides, breechings, and tackles, among other articles, from Black Rock. His lists of property from Buffalo included four 32-pounder long guns, and he told Holdup that if the 32s could not be sent, to send two 24s instead. Although he had a maximum total of twenty-five long guns at his base, he used only sixteen in the action, substituting them with heavier carronades before he went into battle. Thus, when he was ready for battle it was notable that he reduced his long gun battery on his main brigs to increase his carronade battery. He obviously wanted a close-range action, which made sense for his chances given his armament.[15] For him it was a critical choice, but a choice which won him the battle.

Barclay, as well, was faced with some critical choices. He faced a shortage of stores; he faced an enemy with a shipbuilding advantage; he was unimpressed with the quality of his crew; he had a shortage of seamen for his squadron; his new vessel *Detroit* was slow in being built; and he was deficient in small transport craft. Luck seemed to have deserted him when he missed Perry's Black Rock division of schooners in the fog; he found that he had to wait for the arrival of small vessels from Lake Huron to transport the artillery and troops; and he had to rely on a blockade of Perry's forces, which failed. He also considered "it will require at least from 250 to 300 seamen to render His Majesty's Squadron perfectly effective."[16] His lack of trained seamen placed him at a *tactical* disadvantage. Sir George Prevost had tried to press Admiral Sir John Borlase Warren, commanding officer of the North American station, for seamen for the lakes. On June 24, he wrote of Lake Erie, "where Captain Barclay is gone to command and whose wants on this Head as he has lately very feelingly described to me, are great and pressing."[17] Barclay continued to press for extra men. His position had not improved in that regard in the three weeks from June 28, when he listed the American forces as two brigs or corvettes, seven schooners, and two smaller brigs, one of them being the captured *Caledonia.*[18] And yet, despite the lack of skilled seamen, Barclay began to prepare for an attack by embarking artillery in his ships.

In the last few days before the battle took place, General Henry Procter at Amherstburg reported that Barclay was exercising the men at the guns and that offensive operations would start when the anticipated seamen arrived. He cautioned, "I must say, because I know it to be the Case, that the Supply of both Officers and Seamen is very inadequate." Barclay also indicated that he expected to meet the American squadron, though he had no idea of its movements, for he sent out only a canoe to search for them, as he was afraid that a sudden calm, and the ability of the American schooners to use sweeps, would mean an increase of their force at the expense of his own. Barclay judged the arrival of seamen to be essential and explained to Yeo that "by dint of exercising the Soldiers on board I hope they will make a good hand of it, when they are backed by a few Seamen. I hope you will add to this gang from the *Dover,* as they will be a small reinforcement of themselves however valuable even a small number is."[19]

Barclay's armament problem was most closely linked to the need to arm the *Detroit* after its armament had been destroyed by Chauncey in the York raid. It was eventually resolved by stripping the fort at Malden of its artillery, and the army of most of its artillery. On August 19, Procter wrote that the squadron was manned and the *Detroit* armed. On the twenty-sixth, he mentioned that all of his ordnance "except the Field (guns)" was on board the squadron,[20] which was why he was so apprehensive about a disaster for the squadron from want of seamen to man it effectively. Barclay decided to wait until seamen might arrive, or, at least, were discovered to be on their way. Only two alternatives presented themselves if this first course proved fruitless. He could either retreat with the army after burning his vessels, or risk an action in the hope of gaining the victory despite the odds. Barclay considered the latter to be the only honorable alternative and decided to risk everything rather than abandon his vessels without a struggle. He had Procter's full approval for this, and, as it happened, he anticipated Prevost's orders to the same effect.[21] As he did, however, he was taking a squadron fully 50 percent inferior in fire power into action. What kind of action could Barclay thus control?

In fighting the Lake Erie battle, Perry possessed an enormous advantage, even though the sum total of his guns was fewer than Barclay's. Perry had at least sixty-five guns, possibly more, shipped to Erie: thirty-six from Washington, some from New York, and more from Sacket's Harbor. These guns—three 32-pound long guns, forty 32-pound short carronades, five 24-pound long guns, two 18-pound long guns, and fifteen 12-pound long guns—totalled sixty-five, together with 6,024 pounds of shot. Fifty-five of these guns were on his ships in the action of September 10. On each of Perry's two large brigs were eighteen 32-pounder carronades and two long 12s. His smaller vessels carried mainly heavy long guns. The *Caledonia* had two long 24s and a 32-pounder carronade. The schooners carried between them three long 32s, two long 24s, four long 12s, two 32-pounder carronades, and two small swivels, not listed in his armament at the end of the action, but evidently small 3s.[22] As most of the guns in the schooners and in the *Caledonia* were pivot guns, and as only the broadsides on the *Lawrence* and the *Niagara* represented half of their total guns, Perry's squadron threw much more in broadside than 50 percent of the sum total of his armament. This was the crucial safety margin which allowed Perry to win a badly fought battle.

There is little doubt that Perry had a squadron greatly superior in firepower. Perry's and Barclay's forces, as they possessed them on the day of the battle, are enumerated in tables 1 and 2.

Historians of this action have had mixed results in seeking to determine the guns' strengths. Mahan thought it impossible to say what the weight of the *Detroit*'s battery was in broadside, though he believed the vessel fired in total 230 pounds. He was 22 pounds short, for the sum total of Barclay's fire power was 252 pounds. Mahan added that "it is incredible that a seaman like Barclay should not have disposed them as to give more than half that amount to one broadside."[23] Mahan was over-analyzing at this point; how could Barclay have known which would have been his engaged side, in the event of a wind shift? He would have had to keep a relatively balanced broadside on each side. Despite Mahan's speculations to the contrary, it is possible, however, to work out the limits of what Barclay's broadside could have been, and what it probably was. Perry observed there was one pivot gun on board the *Detroit*. Roosevelt assumed this to be one of the 24s, and he divided the remainder by two (six 12s, eight 9s, which equals in broadside three 12s and four 9s), and offset the two short guns, the 24 and the 18, by the long guns of the same caliber. With the 24 as the pivot, this would give a broadside of 138 pounds.[24] William James described the pivot guns in the British squadron as one 18, two 12s, and two 9s,[25] so that according to James's account, the 18-pound long gun would appear to be the pivot gun, leaving one long 24 in each broadside with the 24-pound carronade on the side, offsetting the 18-pound carronade on the other.

If Mahan's point about the heavier guns being most likely on the engaged side is accepted, it must be seriously qualified. Barclay would not have left one side of his flagship with 168 pounds and the other with only 84 (one 12 and eight 9s), even if the 18-pounder pivot would have increased that side to 102; for it was not apparent, as he ran down towards the Bass Islands under easy canvas, which would be the principal engaged side. It is probable, therefore, that 9- and 12-pounder guns were fairly evenly divided on either side before he left Amherstburg, for he did not know who would have the weather gage in the action. The choice of position dictated by wind and the approach of the

Table 1

Perry's Squadron on September 10

Vessel Name	*Tons*	*Guns*	*Calibre*	*Crew Total*	*Metal Total*	*Broadside*
Lawrence	492.6	18 2	32 cdes 12s	142	576 24	300
Niagara	492.6	18 2	32 cdes 12s	137	576 24	300
Caledonia	85	3	2 24s 1 32	48	80	80
Ariel	63	4	12s pivots	40		
Scorpion	63	2	1 32; 1 24 cde on pivots	29		
Tigress	52	1	32 pivot	18	256	256
Porcupine	52	1	32	27		
Somers	86	2	1 24; 1 32 cde swivels	27		
Trippe	63	1	1 32	38		
TOTALS	1449.2	54		506	1536	936
Did not participate in battle:						
Ohio (NIA)	62	2	24		48	
Amelia (condemned)	72	1	24		24	
Reserve Guns		7	12s		84	
TOTALS	1583.2	64			1692	

Source: Based on "Statement of the Force of the United States Squadron September 10," Perry Papers.

enemy might have meant either broadside could have been required in the impending action. If one accepts this even distribution, then the problem that exists is caused by the distribution of Barclay's bigger guns. In addition, because of his lack of good seamen, he had to have his guns already well secured and roped into place before he left harbor. He was seaman enough to arrange his guns so that the complex task of bringing ammunition to the infantrymen who were serving them would not be complicated by alternating different bores and caliber; that would have been too confusing for raw gunners. Thus, it is more than likely that his 12s and his 9s were in rank together, not alternated, and arranged evenly with similar numbers on either side. The only clue is that Barclay stated he commenced the action by "firing a few long guns"[26] which suggests immediately his 18 and 24s, possibly in the bow. The smaller guns may not have carried as far and would have been closer to the stern or midships.

The total maximum broadside Barclay could have engaged would have been 168 pounds, three 24s (two long, one carronade), two 18s (one long, one carronade), and five 12s; but that would have been an unprofessional, if not downright silly, distribution that would have left only 84 pounds on the other side.[27] Depending on the distribution of guns, broadside figures of 168, 165, 162, 159, 156, 153, 150, 147, 144, 141, and 138 are possible weights of the metal thrown from one broadside. Discarding the three upward extremes for the reason that Barclay would not have overpacked one side and seriously diminished the other to such an extent, one is left with the probability that his range of broadside in the action lay between 159 and 138 pounds. Any closer estimate has to be a guess, and the 138 looks to be the best based on the following distribution: the 18-pounder pivot, with two 24s, three 12s, and four 9s. This would leave the same 18-pounder pivot (which counted double duty, of course), one 24, and one 18 with three 12s and four 9s opposite, for a total of 132 pounds on his nonengaged side.

The *Queen Charlotte*'s broadside is easier to evaluate. She fired fourteen 24-pounder carronades and three long 12s (possibly 9s), one a pivot (a total of 372 pounds). Thus she had seven 24-pounder carronades, a long 12 in broadside, with another 12-pounder pivot in broadside, for nine guns throwing 192 pounds in broadside. Her total armament of 372 pounds made her the most heavily armed ship that the British possessed. However, her guns had not the range of the *Detroit*'s long guns, for they were carronades lighter than Perry's, and therein lay a problem. Should Barclay have fought a long-gun action by sheering away from Perry's impending force and thereby nullifying the *Queen Charlotte*'s smaller carronades? Or should he have expected the close action he did fight and thus distribute beforehand some of the *Queen Charlotte*'s carronades onto the *Detroit* in return for some of the *Detroit*'s long guns? This would have given each main vessel of the British squadron a more balanced weight of broadside metal relative to the opposition.

Table 2

Barclay's Squadron on September 10

Vessel Name	*Guns*	*Calibre*	*Crew Total*	*Metal Total*	*Broadside*
Detroit Ship	19	2 24 pdr 1 18 pdr (1 pivot) 6 12 pdr 8 9 pdr 1 24 pdr cde 1 18 pdr cde	160	252	138
Queen Charlotte Ship	17	3 12s (9s?) (1 pivot) 14 24 cdes	110	372	192
Lady Prevost Schooner	13	10 12 cdes & 3 long 9s (1 pivot)	76	147	78
General Hunter Brig	10	2 6s 4 4s 2 2s 2 12s	39	56	28
Chippewa Schooner	1	1 travsg long 12 pdr 1 12 pdr cde	25	24	24
Little Belt Sloop	3	1 travsg (long 12 pdr & 1 24 pdr cde)	15	36	36
TOTALS	63		425	887	496

Source: Armament of the British squadron, Lieutenant Francis Purvis of the *Detroit* to the court, Barclay Court Martial, 9 September 1814, Public Records Office, London, Adm 1/5445, pp. 21–22.

Note: See also Wood, *Select Documents* 2:315. The two swivels are mentioned by Perry in his "Statement of the British force in the action of September 10," 13 September 1813, in the Perry Papers, copy in *Niles Weekly Register* 5:62, and *American State Papers Naval Affairs* 1:297.

The *General Hunter*'s small "pop-guns," as Mahan termed them,[28] though ten in number, threw only fifty-six pounds altogether, twenty-eight in broadside. Not one of the *Hunter*'s guns could really be labeled as one of Michael Lewis's "ship-killers" though the 6-pounders could have inflicted some damage on Perry's slighter vessels. Should the *Hunter* have been fought at all, or should she have been removed and her crew distributed onto the ships and the *Lady Prevost* which had a 9-pounder pivot and two fixed 9s as well as her ten 12-pounder carronades (so her broadside was 78 pounds)? The *Chippewa* and *Little Belt* threw 24 and 35 pounds respectively, hardly ship-killing efforts. Perry claimed the *Chippewa* had two pivots,[29] like the *Somers* of his own squadron, of unknown caliber. If one assumes the *Detroit*'s broadside was 138, then Barclay's broadside was 138 (*Detroit*), 192 (*Queen Charlotte*), 28 (*Hunter*), 78 (*Lady Prevost*), 24 (*Chippewa*), and 36 (*Little Belt*); a total of 496 pounds with over 67 percent broadside metal thrown from his two large ships and 82 percent from his first three.

Gun strengths in total and broadside weight reveal the dilemma for Barclay. At his Presque Isle base, Perry's ordnance stores contained at least twenty-five long guns and forty carronades. The potential battering strength of Perry's long guns thus totaled 484 pounds and his carronades totaled *at least* 1,184/1,208 pounds of fire power. In the action of the 10th, he used sixteen long guns totaling 328 pounds and thirty-eight carronades totaling 1,208 pounds. Mainly because of pivot guns, Perry's broadside strength was 304 long-gun pounds and 632 pounds of carronades, totaling 936. On his ships, therefore, Perry's weight of broadside metal was 576 pounds from the carronades of the two large brigs, 96 pounds from the three pivot carronades in the schooners, and 264 pounds from the long guns in the schooners and the two long guns in the large brigs (936).

Barclay, on the other hand, used in the action thirty-three long guns totaling 353 pounds of firepower, and twenty-eight carronades totaling 534 pounds of battery power. In broadside, however, Barclay had 208 pounds of long-gun metal and 288 pounds of carronade metal, totaling 496 pounds in broadside. Thus, ironically, although Perry's total long-gun strength of 328 was close to Barclay's total long-gun strength of 353, and though Barclay had nineteen or twenty long guns to Perry's eleven in broadside, yet, mainly because of the pivots, Perry's vessels threw 304 pounds of long-gun broadside metal to Barclay's 178 pounds. Barclay had thus only 58.5 percent of Perry's *long gun broadside* force. Turning to total carronade battering strength in the action, Barclay's carronade metal was 534 pounds to Perry's 1,208, or only 44.2 percent of

Perry's total carronades. In *broadside carronade* strength Barclay's fourteen carronades threw 288 pounds of carronade metal contrasted to Perry's twenty-one guns firing 632 pounds, a factor of 45.5 percent of Perry's force.

When adding the long-gun metal and the carronade metal together, Perry's total of 1,536, compared with Barclay's total of 887, meant that Barclay had only 57.7 percent of Perry's *total firepower*. When comparing broadsides, however, where pivot guns can be used on either side of the vessel, the percentages alter slightly. In long guns, Barclay was deficient at 58.5 percent of Perry's force, a factor of 3 to 5, and in carronades he had only 45.5 percent of Perry's force, a factor just over 2 to 5. Adding both guns and carronades together *in broadside,* he was thus inferior by 52.9 percent of Perry's force (496 pounds to 936), or a factor of 1:2. Quite simply, Barclay's squadron was inferior in firepower by almost 50 percent.[30] When Barclay sailed into battle he had odds against him of 5 to 3 in long guns and 5 to 2 in carronades.

Was Barclay inevitably doomed? Should he have fought a close-action fight on September 10? The initial answer would be no! His action in forcing the *Lawrence,* Perry's flagship, to strike was, if you calculate the odds, one of the most significant ship achievements in the war. But a short-range, close action, given the nature of his guns, their range, their inadequate broadside power compared with Perry's defensive power and the offensive power of his brigs, made the odds so great that Barclay's naval tactics in seeking a close-action encounter contributed to his defeat. Could he have won at all in the action fought on the 10th? Probably not, given the gun disparity, unless the bottom had dropped out of the *Niagara,* for Perry fought a divided action and still won. Could he have won at all in *any* kind of action? It is possible that if he had tried for a running fight, dragged over a large expanse of lake, he may have had more of a chance if his opponent's squadron had sailed badly. A battle at long range would have given him greater odds; one at short range would not, and that depended upon who had the weather gage. When the weather gage swung to Perry before the action commenced, and allowed him to pick the speed of approach and shorten the range of engagement, the odds of Barclay's winning immediately diminished, and the difference between his and Perry's armament was reduced from 5:3 against to 5:2 against in gun strength alone.

Could Barclay have fought an action to board? Hardly in the conditions of September 10, without the weather gage. The irony, of course, was that he did not have the sailors to sail his vessels for such a running meeting, nor the seamen to maneuver to board from his two main ships after the pounding given and taken by the *Lawrence.* It is unnecessary speculation to assume that had he survived unwounded, as Perry did, he might have been able to ensure that the *Detroit* and *Queen Charlotte* could have avoided falling foul of one another and thus prolonged the struggle by swinging his vessels to meet the fresh *Niagara.* He had not the supplies to keep up a skirmishing and long-running disengagement and his squadron was not tested as to whether it sailed faster than Perry's. Perry put most of his eggs in his boats' armament (it was Mahan who called gun brigs "egg shells armed with hammers") and adopted the tactics of ship-killing for victory. Barclay, on the other hand, had no such tactical choices. Short of sailors, short of an adequate ship-killing armament to meet a new and powerful brig with unimpaired powers of resistance, and with his two main ships crippled, Barclay was damned if he fought a close action, damned if he ranged in a running fight, and damned if he had not fought at all.

W. A. B. DOUGLAS

The Honor of the Flag Had Not Suffered: Robert Heriot Barclay and the Battle of Lake Erie

Robert Heriot Barclay, who was the loser in the Battle of Put-in-Bay, and William Bell, the master shipwright who built the ships sailing under Barclay's command, have remained shadowy figures in the history books. We remember Barclay's counterpart, Oliver Hazard Perry, as a great naval hero. By the time of the battle's centennial in 1913, much had also been made of Daniel Dobbins, the shipwright from Erie, who persuaded the navy to set up its base there.[1] When Howard Chapelle published his history of the American sailing navy in 1949, he brought out the similar importance of those wonderful shipbuilders, Henry Eckford and Adam and Noah Brown.[2] There has been much less about Barclay in standard accounts of the period, little about the men he commanded, and almost nothing about Bell. The purpose of this discussion is to focus mostly on Barclay.

American historians give Barclay his due. "The heroic Barclay," wrote Alfred Thayer Mahan:

> not only had borne himself gallantly and tenaciously against a superior force—favored in so doing by the enemy attacking in detail—but the testimony on his trial showed that he had labored diligently during the brief period of his command, amid surroundings of extreme difficulty, to equip his squadron, and to train to discipline and efficiency the heterogeneous material of which his crews were composed.[3]

Whatever mistakes Barclay might have made, said Mahan, "the honor of the flag had not suffered."

Theodore Roosevelt says that Barclay's account of the battle "is a model of its kind for candor and generosity," and,

> in spite of the amount of boasting it has given rise to, I should say it was a battle to be looked upon as in an equally high degree creditable to both sides. Indeed, if it were not for the fact that the victory was so complete, it might be said that the length of the contest and the trifling disparity in loss reflected rather the most credit on the British.[4]

He goes on to make a statement about the relative merits of Old Englanders and New Englanders:

> The only un-English element in the contest was the presence among the Canadian English of some of the descendants of the Latin race from whom they had conquered the country. Otherwise, the men were equally matched; but the Americans owed their success . . . to the fact that their officers had been trained in the best and most practical, although the smallest, navy of the day. The British sailors on the lakes were as good as our own, but no better.[5]

Roosevelt was, I think, close to the mark in everything but his belief in French Canadian inferiority. That reflects a superficial knowledge, not only of Upper Canadian realities in 1813, but of Barclay himself. Roosevelt's comments were based purely on an assessment of Barclay's performance in 1813. Mahan's knowledge was not much more extensive. He knew Barclay had fought at the Battle of Trafalgar, but little else. Some historians said Barclay was "old and experienced."[6] (He was twenty-seven.) But if Perry is to merit the appellation of hero, it is important to establish a degree of difficulty in overcoming his opposition. The praise lavished upon Barclay by American historians, therefore, is not entirely devoid of selfish motive.

Barclay's contemporaries certainly thought him a very brave man. General Sir George Prevost, governor general and commander in chief in the Canadas, issued a General Order on November 24, 1813, that said, "Captain Barclay and his men have, by their gallant daring, and self-devotion to their country's cause, rescued its honor and their own, even in defeat."[7] Following this lead the people of Quebec asked Barclay to accept a presentation of plate valued at one hundred guineas. After the court-martial, which concluded, "the Judgment and Gallantry of Captain Barclay in taking his Squadron into Action and during the Contest were highly conspicuous and entitled him to the highest praise," the Canada merchants in London, according to the entry in John Marshall's *Royal Naval Biography:*

> voted an increase of 400 guineas to the sum already subscribed by the inhabitants of Quebec, for the purchase of plate to be presented to Captain Barclay. On one of the largest pieces, the following inscription is engraved: "Presented to Captain Robert H. Barclay, of His Majesty's Royal Navy, by the inhabitants of Quebec, in testimony of the sense they justly entertain of the exalted courage and heroic valor displayed by him, and by the officers, seamen and soldiers, of the flotilla under his command, in an action with a greatly superior force of the enemy, upon Lake Erie, on the 10th day of September, 1813; when the presence of a few additional seamen was only wanting to have effected the total discomfiture of the hostile squadron. Of Captain Barclay it may truly be said, that although he could not command victory, he did more—he nobly deserved it!"[8]

This information almost certainly came to Marshall from Barclay himself—the naval biographical collections of the day depended on contributions from the subject—and it is instructive to read on: "On another large piece, an inscription is likewise engraved, expressive of the sentiments of the Canada merchants in London, whose spontaneous mark of their sense of Captain Barclay's zeal in the execution of his duty, could not but be most highly gratifying to him—because, in his defeat their interest was most deeply involved."[9]

That was presumably Barclay's own view of the matter. A view from quite another standpoint comes from Barclay's immediate superior, Commodore Sir James Lucas Yeo, in the letter reporting the action to the Admiralty, dated October 10, 1813 (at least eleven years before Marshall's naval biography came out):

> Notwithstanding, the immense disparity of force, which scarcely left a hope of success, Captain Barclay did not hesitate a moment, but Heroically devoted himself, and the Squadron entrusted to his charge, to the safety of the Army, the preservation of the Province and, what was equally dear to him, the Honor of the British Flag.[10]

But Yeo was laying the groundwork for protecting his decisions, casting doubt on those of army commanders in the Canadas, and preparing the way for his letter of November 14, in which he was to write: "I fear that Captain Barclay acted under the impression that if successful he had everything to gain; and if not, little to lose."[11] Barclay clearly had less regard for Yeo's praise than that of his mercantile benefactors. Yet the phrase, "Honor of the Flag," is prominent once again. Barclay had not forfeited the respect of his peers.

This was evident fifty years later in the words of the loyalist William H. Coffin, in his *1812: The War and its Moral.* He first cites James Fenimore Cooper: "The hardy frontiermen of the American lakes are as able to endure fatigue, as ready to engage, and as constant in battle, as the seamen of any marine in the world. They merely require good leaders, and these the English appear to have possessed in Captain Barclay and his assistants." Then Coffin writes:

> Barclay was the type of a British sailor. He had served under Nelson. He was noted for personal courage, and for that moral courage which, at the call of duty, defies despair. He was one of those sea-dogs which looses its hold only in death. He expected more from human nature than could be found in any other nature than his own. His dispatch [about the battle] does not do justice to the brave men who stood by him so truly.
>
> Some months afterwards, he tottered before a court-martial, like a Roman trophy—nothing but helm and hauberk. He had lost an arm at Trafalgar [this was wrong; Barclay lost his right arm as the result of a convoy battle in 1809 in the English Channel, but the error found its way into subsequent accounts, such as Mahan's]; the other rendered useless by grape shot through the shoulder. He was further weakened by several severe flesh wounds. Little wonder, that men not given to such weakness shed tears at the spectacle. Little wonder, that the president of the court, in returning his sword, told him, in a voice tremulous with emotion, that the conduct of his men had been most honorable to themselves and to their country.[12]

Coffin's reference to "the brave men who stood by" Barclay is worth noting. It will be dealt with later. For the moment, it is enough to observe that historians and contemporaries agree about Barclay's bravery and tactical skill in battle. Clearly, from all the secondary accounts, Barclay's one lapse was to let Perry and his ships escape out of Erie and into the lake during the summer of 1813. Because they cannot find out why he did it, historians give him the benefit of the doubt. Mahan said he was simply out-generalled. The Canadian historian E. A. Cruikshank says (on no apparent evidence but in contradiction to local mythology) that the weather was unsuitable; he was low in stores; and he had to take his ships over the bar at the entrance to Erie harbor. Perry's biographer, James Cook Mills, argues that Barclay decided not to engage Perry's ships, even as they came out of the harbor, because he wanted to have the new ship then under construction (*Detroit*) ready before he went into battle. Of all the explanations this seems the most likely, if we can believe the memory of Daniel Dobbins.[13]

Dobbins pointed out that on August 4, when Barclay returned to Erie to look into the harbor, the wind was from the southeast and the shoreline obscured by haze. Barclay could see all the ships but *Lawrence* out and laying at anchor in formation. *Lawrence* was hard aground on the bar, but that would not have been apparent to an observer in the offing, and it would have appeared as if Perry was out in force, ready to do battle. Dobbins says he learned after the battle from Charles Frederic Rolette, of whom more later, that this was indeed the case, and that Barclay did for this reason decide to postpone battle until *Detroit* was ready.[14]

The loyalists on the north shore of Lake Erie, who suffered the most from Barclay's defeat, did not forgive him so easily. The defeat exposed these refugees from the American Revolution once again to the harassment that had driven them from their homes south of the border. One of them was Amelia Ryerse. In 1813 she was a young girl, too young to have experienced the hardships of the Revolutionary War herself, but only a generation removed. Her uncle was Egerton Ryerson, the notable Canadian churchman and historian of the American loyalists; her father's name had been misspelled in regimental muster lists. Sixty-five years after the events of 1813, when she was Amelia Harris, widow of another British naval officer, and the chatelaine of Eldon House in London, Ontario, her facile pen recorded the facts she remembered.[15] Bitter memories allowed to fester so long are suspect, but what gives this version a smattering of credibility is the statement by Benjamin Lossing, in his *Field Book of the War of 1812,* that he had heard a similar story from Daniel Dobbins, who in turn said he had heard the story from Amelia Ryerse.[16] Her version, published by Ryerson in his history of the American loyalists, therefore, deserves extensive quotation:

> During the summer Captain Barclay used to have private information—not very reliable, as the result proved—of what progress the ships were making on the stocks. He used, occasionally, to leave the blockade and go to Amherstburg and came to Ryerse (near Dover). The Americans took note of this, and made their plans and preparations for doing so. There was a pretty widow of an officer of some rank in Amherstburg, who was very anxious to go to Toronto. Captain Barclay offered her a passage in his ship and brought her to Ryerse, and then escorted her to Dr. Rolph's where he and some of the officers remained to dinner the following day. . . .
>
> No one could have fought more bravely than Captain Barclay. At the same time, those who knew of his leaving the blockade could not help feeling that all the disasters of the upper part of the province lay at his door.

Lossing's version based on hearsay from Daniel Dobbins—and Lossing's book was published eleven years before Egerton Ryerson's, so we may assume the story had been going the rounds for a long time before that—was that Barclay raised the blockade to attend a public dinner offered by residents of Dover. At the dinner Barclay is supposed to have exclaimed, "I expect to find the Yankee brigs hard and fast on the bar at Erie when I return, in which predicament it will be but a small job to destroy them."[17]

It is on the basis of these stories that the Canadian yachtsman and journalist, C. H. J. Snider, wrote about Barclay and the struggle for Lake Erie.[18] Snider did more than almost anyone else to arouse popular interest in the history of Canada's maritime heritage with the books he wrote, mostly for boys, in the early years of this century. In the Canadian tradition, then, Barclay has a mixed reputation. Brave and not too bright might be a fair summary.[19]

As always the truth, so far as we can determine it, lies somewhere between the extremes of these subjective views. It is important to remember that Lake Erie was low on the scale of priorities for both British and American naval commanders on Lake Ontario. Perry came to Lake Erie because he was frustrated at the ineffectiveness of the gunboats he commanded on the Atlantic coast. Barclay came because he was not one of Commodore Yeo's own protégés.

"This command," he explained at his court-martial, was "offered to Captain [William Howe] Mulcaster the next in command to Sir James Yeo, who to my personal knowledge declined it in consequence of its ineffectual state and Sir James Yeo refusing to send seamen." Barclay also drew attention to the personnel given him when he set out for Lake Erie in May 1813, which comprised three lieutenants, one surgeon, one purser, one master's mate, and nineteen men. Barclay continued "12 of these were Canadians who had been discharged from [Yeo's] own squadron on Lake Ontario, the others were the most worthless Characters that came from England with him which can be proved by the Evidence present."[20]

When he arrived at Amherstburg on June 17, Barclay wrote urging an attack on Presque Isle and naval reinforcements for Lake Erie. Yeo sent him "a captain [Lieutenant Finnis] and his servant—no one else. And I beg leave to state to the court that this Letter called forth a reprimand from the Commodore which he stated as being much too peremptory from a Junior to an Officer so much higher in rank." Barclay was only a lieutenant, with the acting rank of commander while holding the Lake Erie appointment, but it rankled that his judgment had been so rudely scorned. He was aware that his exceptional professional abilities had been noted at Trafalgar, when as an acting lieutenant in the *Swiftsure* he rescued 170 French seamen from the *Redoubtable.* He had shown a high order of bravery and skill as second lieutenant in the frigate *Diana,* in the English channel in 1808–09. In 1810 he had gone to the North American station apparently led to believe he would be given a commander's appointment. "Unfortunately for him," explains Marshall's naval biography, again making us privy to Barclay's own view of events, "a change soon took place in the naval administration, and four more years elapsed before he obtained advancement." Had he been one of the officers selected by Yeo, things might have been different. As it was, like other officers who had been sent to the lakes from Bermuda rather than with Yeo from England, he had to contend with conflicting interests, and would not be confirmed in rank until after the Battle of Lake Erie.[21]

The criticism of Barclay's blockading techniques is understandable but not wholly justified. Cruikshank's justification, as has been suggested, cannot be backed up with evidence. The fact is, however, that blockade in this case did not require continual cruising in sight of the enemy's harbor. Barclay underestimated Perry's ability to get his large ships over the bar; the methods used were certainly a surprise to him. It is also certain that until fifty seamen arrived from Lake Ontario in August, Barclay did not have well-trained gun crews in his ships. How they would have fared attempting to take on Perry's ships at anchor under the shelter of shore batteries is a moot question. Captain George Downie at the Battle of Plattsburg in 1815 was totally defeated by the American squadron on Lake Champlain under precisely those kind of conditions. Barclay, in other words, was equipped to watch but not to defeat a squadron of equal or superior force at the time that Perry got his ships onto the lake. When Barclay finally met Perry's squadron, there is no question he had, by constant gun drill, improved the fighting capabilities of his force immeasurably; and had circumstances favored him just a little more, it seems entirely likely, with the fifty seamen at last sent to him, that he would have won the day on September 10.[22]

Not until relatively recent years did anyone bother to find out what happened to Barclay after the War of 1812.[23] This has not found its way to any new history of the Battle of Lake Erie, American, British, or Canadian; yet it is important because it shows that in the Royal Navy, losers did not prosper. Barclay received his confirmation in the rank of commander after the battle, but never again found significant employment in the service. In February 1822, he wrote to Sir John J. Douglas, a friend in Whitehall, for advice about soliciting the patronage of the

Duke of Buckingham whose speech in the House of Lords in 1814 about his defeat, Barclay thought, was responsible for his loss of interest and consequent promotion.

> I should be sorry to suspect that his Grace would be loath to do me an act of justice and generosity to do away with an injury which he never could intend, but yet which has attached itself to me with singular pertinacity: which has deprived me of 5 years rank, of a [illegible] of pension, and of being placed on a level with my compeers on the Lake Service; of whom not one could show more service to merit their promotion than I could. My duty to myself and my family and friends, my sense of the cruel exception taken to my position and services, all confirm in an irresistable manner in making me most anxious to be placed on the list of Post Captains; and my conduct on former occasions some of which you have yourself witnessed, and the multitude of severity of my wounds received in the honourable discharge of my professional duty may live as a strong assurance to the Duke of Buckingham and those who may instruct themselves, for me, that if occasion again offers I shall not disgrace their kindness.[24]

Barclay was not being quite straightforward. He had previously petitioned for a pension, and after the mandatory wait of a year and a day from his court-martial, the College of Surgeons having confirmed that his wounds, added to the loss of a limb, continued to be prejudicial to his health, he was granted a pension of two hundred pounds in addition to the five pence a day he was already receiving. However, his letters evidently found their mark, for on October 14, 1824, he was appointed to the bomb vessel *Infernal,* and stayed there for about eight months. This was enough to qualify him for the rank of post captain. In 1831, we find that Barclay, who had married Agnes Cosser of Millbank Street, Westminster, in 1814, and by now had several sons and daughters, received a pension of four hundred pounds. So although his naval career had effectively come to an end after the War of 1812, he was not without financial security.[25]

The same could not be said of the provincial marine officers who took part in the Battle of Lake Erie. Before Barclay arrived on the scene, it is true, the Provincial Marine lacked professional naval leadership. Barclay gave Captain G. B. Hall, his predecessor in command on the lake, short shrift, and was only prepared to accept his service under command of an officer in the Royal Navy. Hall refused these terms and went ashore, ending up with an appointment in the shore establishment of the lakes. The most impressive of Hall's officers was Charles Frederic Rolette, who had captured, among a large number of American prizes, the vessel containing Hull's dispatches in 1812, thus playing an important part in Sir Isaac Brock's defeat of the American general. During the Battle of Lake Erie, Rolette was first lieutenant of the *Lady Prevost,* taking command when Lieutenant Buchan of the Royal Navy was mortally wounded. He fought the ship "with great skill and heroic gallantry until being severely wounded in the right side and seriously burnt by an explosion of gunpowder, which killed and wounded a number of his men, he surrendered his ship an unmanageable and sinking wreck."[26] After undergoing a year as a prisoner of war, he returned to his native Quebec where the citizens presented him a sword of honor worth fifty-six guineas. In 1817 he received a grant of twelve hundred acres in recognition of his services, but Rolette never recovered from his wounds, and became involved in litigation over his property which had not been resolved when he died at the age of forty-six. Death relieved him of suffering he had accepted with patience and resignation, but it also left a widow and six children in a state of poverty. Luce Rolette's subsequent petitions for a widow's pension continued for ten years.[27]

The other provincial marine officer whose name appears prominently in accounts of the battle is Lieutenant Robert Irvine, whose inexperience led to the fatal shiphandling mistake that gave Perry his advantage over the *Queen Charlotte* and *Detroit* at the crucial moment of the engagement. Irvine was never faulted for his bravery. William Coffin represented the Canadian loyalist view, however, in taking exception to the mild criticism Barclay levelled at this provincial marine officer. Irvine's subsequent life is something of a mystery, but it appears he had changed his name owing to some circumstance in his earlier life. He, too, received twelve hundred acres and presumably was able to take advantage of the grant. We remember Irvine best for his accurate representation, in a remarkable painting, of the ships involved in the Battle of Lake Erie.[28]

Contemporary accounts and historical analyses alike have devoted so much attention to "The Honour of the Flag" that, in spite of the fact that an important article in the *Mariner's Mirror* accurately called the War of 1812 on the lakes a shipbuilder's war, the master shipwright responsible for building Barclay's squadron has been ignored.

William Bell had been in Amherstburg since the turn of the century and went on to become a successful shipbuilder in Quebec after the war. Like Henry Eckford, one of his American counterparts, he had Scottish origins and learned his trade in Quebec.[29] Between June 1799 and September 1813, he built the snow *Earl Camden* (16 guns), the schooner

General Hope (12), the brig *General Hunter* (10), the ship *Queen Charlotte* (18), the schooner *Lady Prevost* (12), and the ship *Detroit* (18), besides a number of gunboats. His efforts ensured that the *Detroit* was ready for Barclay's use in September 1813, even though the guns had to be taken from the ramparts of Fort Malden and the sails were the spare set for *Queen Charlotte.* Perry's great achievement in building a fleet on Lake Erie depended on the ability of remarkable shipwrights, using great ingenuity to exploit a wealth of resources and naval stores. Barclay depended on one highly skillful master of the shipwright's trade, using comparable ingenuity to make do with almost no resources but timber from the primeval forest. Except for passing mention in some articles, Bell has never received his due.[30]

After the battle, when General Harrison advanced up the Thames River, Bell (who claimed he was wounded during the capture of Amherstburg) escaped with his family, and although he suffered considerable losses, his skills were in demand. He never suffered for employment during the war. After arriving at Kingston in October 1813, he was put in charge of the dockyard and superintended the building of the *Prince Regent* (56), *Prince Charlotte* (36), *St. Lawrence* (112), and the Governor's yacht *Toronto.* On July 24, 1814, Bell was superceded by a master shipwright, Mr. Strickland, who arrived from England with three hundred men; but a year later he returned, having been to England and back, this time "under the navy" rather than the provincial marine, appointed assistant to the master shipbuilder of His Majesty's Naval Yards in Canada. It so happened that Mr. Strickland, at Kingston, was killed by his horse in July 1815, and Bell replaced him until late in 1816, when the naval establishment in the Canadas was reduced. It is pleasant to record that, after bombarding Whitehall with the petitions and memorials common to that age, Bell won a pension from the Lords of Treasury, and went on to prosper in Quebec.[31]

One hundred and seventy-five years after the event, we still look back upon the Battle of Lake Erie, which as naval battles go was a relatively insignificant affair, as a demonstration of human courage and ingenuity. The extent to which both Barclay and Perry depended upon their shipwrights and naval stores has been recognized by historians in recent times; fighting a naval battle in the wilderness was a triumph of technology. But battles, which waste and wreck human lives on the one hand, and create lasting traditions on the other, are (as military historians are wont to assert) just the tip of the iceberg. By the time that the Battle of Lake Erie was fought, it is clear there was a well-established shipping industry on the upper Great Lakes, and that the need for naval forces had done much to stimulate that industry at Amherstburg. After the War of 1812 there was less need in the lakes for such activity. William Bell found better scope for his talents in Quebec. Despite the heroism of the men for whom he labored in 1813, Bell may have been in his own way the most significant individual involved in the Battle of Lake Erie under the British flag. The fact remains—and even in our cynical and materialistic age, we can accept that for Canadians it remains the most important fact about the Battle of Lake Erie—the honor of that flag did not suffer, even in defeat, thanks to Barclay and the men under his command who fought and died for it on September 10, 1813. "It is experiences and memories like these," remarked C. P. Stacey in 1958, "that make nations."[32]

DENNIS CARTER-EDWARDS

The Battle of Lake Erie and Its Consequences: Denouement of the British Right Division and Abandonment of the Western District to American Troops, 1813–1815

On the afternoon of September 10, 1813, Lieutenant Colonel Augustus Warburton, commanding officer of the British forces at Amherstburg, stood on a high point of land at Hartley's Point where the Detroit River entered Lake Erie, watching the British fleet under Captain Robert H. Barclay as it engaged the American fleet commanded by Captain Oliver Hazard Perry. For nearly three hours the two squadrons poured volley after volley of round and canister shot at each other, bringing death and destruction with each broadside. Warburton's first impression of the contest was that the British were victorious as Barclay's flagship *Detroit* succeeded in disabling Perry's ship *Lawrence.* The good news was quickly dispatched to an anxious public back in Amherstburg. However, jubilation turned to despair when it was learned the following day that the entire British fleet had been captured.[1]

The loss of British naval control on Lake Erie set in motion a series of events which led to the precipitous withdrawal of the Right Division from the Detroit frontier, the disastrous defeat at Moraviantown, and the subsequent isolation of this district for the remainder of the war. Thus, the Battle of Lake Erie was the critical factor in this theater in the War of 1812. It brought the tenuous British hold on the Detroit area to a crisis point and laid bare the border for American occupation for the duration of the contest.

The consequences of this occupation of Canadian soil by an American army were devastating for the residents living in the Western District of Upper Canada. As the American garrison attempted to maintain a secure foothold on the Canadian side of the Detroit River, they resorted to increasingly harsh measures to feed and house their troops. Raids into the River Thames area and points further east resulted in the destruction of crops and mills vital to the survival of the residents of this part of the province. Within the towns of Amherstburg and Sandwich, homes were forcibly occupied, livestock taken without payment, and private citizens threatened for offering aid to the enemy. It was these families, along with their homes and farms, that bore the brunt of American military measures during the latter stages of the war. They, as much as the Right Division, suffered defeat and hardship as a result of the Battle of Lake Erie.

President Madison's Declaration of War signed June 18, 1812, cited a list of grievances as justification for his national call to arms. Included in the list of British affronts to the national character were veiled references to the officials of the Indian Department operating out of Fort Amherstburg and their encouragement of Indian raids on the frontier settlements. It was clear this region would see its share of fighting in the ensuing contest.

British mastery over the Detroit frontier was achieved early in the war by Major General Isaac Brock's bold strike against Detroit in August 1812. The surrender of Brigadier General William Hull and the first Army of the Northwest temporarily removed the American threat to this district. Further British victories at Frenchtown in January 1813, and later at Fort Meigs in May that same year, frustrated American efforts to recapture Detroit and drive the British from their base at Amherstburg.

However, by the summer of 1813, the British grip on the territory bordering the American side of the Detroit River was slipping. In August one wing of William Henry Harrison's new army of the Northwest was advancing towards Monroe, Michigan, while the other wing was establishing a secure base near Put-in-Bay, Lake Erie, in anticipation of an amphibious operation against the Western District of Upper Canada.

Lieutenant Colonel Henry Procter, the British commander of the Right Division, not only had to contend with this two-prong advance by enemy troops, but also felt constrained to keep a wary eye on His Britannic Majesty's native allies, who had played such a critical role in the early victories. Local Wyandot, Potawatomi, and Shawnee were reinforced during the summer of 1813 by western tribes brought from Michilimackinac to Amherstburg by the popular Indian agent, Robert Dickson. Procter looked on this augmentation of his force as a mixed blessing. In a blunt dispatch to the commander of the forces, Sir George Prevost, he remarked, "You will perceive that the Indian Force is seldom a disposable one . . . and only found useful in Proportion as we are independent of it."[2]

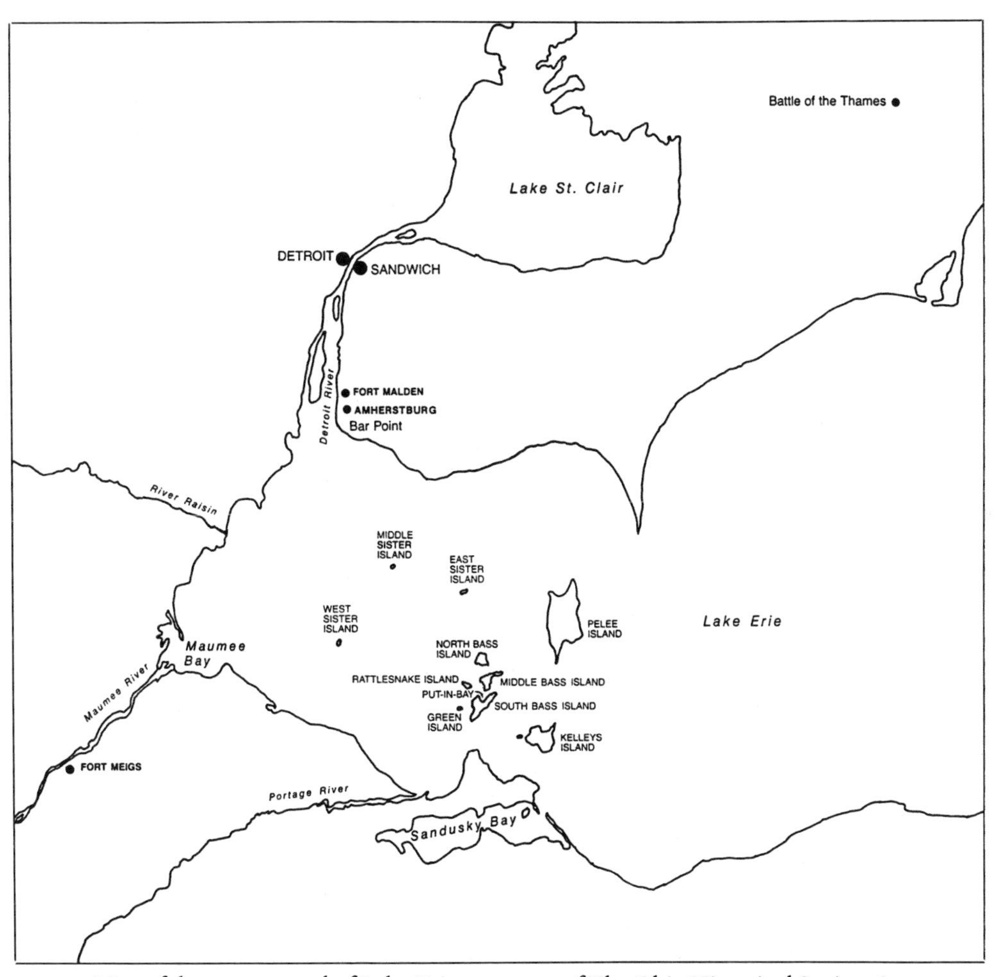

Map of the western end of Lake Erie, courtesy of The Ohio Historical Society/ *Timeline* magazine.

Procter's worst fears about the disproportionate balance between his regular and irregular forces were realized following a disastrous raid against Fort Stephenson in August 1813. The British failure to capture urgently needed supplies of beef and corn and the heavy casualties suffered by the regulars left Procter badly shaken and anxious about his precarious hold on the Indians collected around the post.

As a remedy for this situation, Procter continually pressed Prevost for additional supplies of men, equipment, currency, and food. In mid-

August he wrote, "I must entreat your Excellency to send me more troops. . . . [You] may rely on my best endeavours, but I rely on the troops alone and they are but few."[3] Again that same month, he pleaded with Prevost to "send me the means of continuing the Contest. . . . Your Excellency will find that we will do our duty but I heartily hope for more assistance from you." A note of desperation is evident in Procter's correspondence as he pressed for badly needed assistance while complaining about his chronic shortages and hinting at conspiracies to deprive him of necessary and frequently promised support. In a letter to Prevost's secretary he wrote, "being situated at the end of a long line I do not feel the full effects of His Excellency's consideration for me, the Aid intended never reaches me undiminished, from some circumstance or other."[4] His charge that valuable supplies were being syphoned off at posts such as Niagara was only partially true, for stores intended for Amherstburg had been destroyed during an enemy raid on York in April 1813, and were difficult to replace in such a short period of time.

Procter was not alone in registering his concern over the lack of supplies and manpower. In June 1813, Captain Robert H. Barclay, R.N., arrived at Amherstburg to take charge of the naval establishment, in particular the completion of the flagship *Detroit* which was on the stocks at the government dockyard. Barclay soon lent his voice to the chorus of complaints about shortages. On September 1, he wrote a private note to the senior naval officer, Commodore Sir James Lucas Yeo, about the small number of properly trained marines available to him and the critical shortage of guns and supplies with which to outfit his fleet. As a result, he was forced to use regular soldiers who he hoped would "by dint of exercise . . . make a good hand of it when they are backed by a few seamen."[5] Artillery for the new ship had to be stripped from the walls of the fort, although even here the number of shorter-range carronades was insufficient.

Both Prevost and Yeo were well aware of the precarious position of the British forces on the right wing and took what steps they could to provide assistance. However, as Prevost pointedly reminded Procter, he had many other demands on his limited resources and had to allocate judiciously his troops and equipment. "You cannot be ignorant," he wrote to Procter, "of the limited nature of the force at my disposal for the defense of an extensive frontier and ought therefore not to count too largely upon my disposition to strengthen the right division."[6] Prevost's remarks underscored the relative importance attached to defense of the western frontier by the senior command. Simply put, the principal objective of the war effort was to protect the core district around Montreal and Quebec and, to a lesser extent, Kingston. Certainly a British presence in the west was important to rally the local population and maintain a vital link with native groups, but the allocation of resources indicated the regions' relative significance in the overall conduct of the war.

Despite the cautionary remarks by Prevost, supplies were forwarded to the Western District. In late August, Procter received word that naval carronades for his ships were at Kingston and would soon be at Burlington for transshipment to Amherstburg. Similarly, some fifty trained seamen taken from the British transport *Dover* were also en route from Kingston. Even more dramatic efforts were made to insure a supply of flour to feed the many mouths that Procter constantly complained of. Wagons were commandeered at the head of Lake Ontario to transport barrels of flour by land to the Thames River to relieve the pressure on the local commissary.[7] Although assured of such aid, Procter was losing faith in oft-repeated promises of support. On September 5, the trained seamen from the ship *Dover* finally arrived at Amherstburg. Instead of the fifty men he was promised, Barclay received only thirty-six men with two lieutenants, one master's mate and two gunners. Nor was the desperate food shortage remedied. An unusually warm summer rendered many of the area grist mills inoperative, forcing the commissariat officer to substitute potatoes for flour when issuing rations to the men.[8]

Yet Procter's main concern was not the troops but rather the native allies and their families who were collected around Fort Amherstburg. This desperate situation was later recalled by Robert Gilmour, the officer responsible for the commissary in testimony presented at Barclay's court-martial:

> The number of Indians including men, women and children were at that time about 14,000 and for some time they had been very clamorous for Provisions. . . . They had already killed working Oxen, Milk cows, Hogs, Sheep and even Dogs belonging to the inhabitants. . . . They [the Indians] had waited upon me threatening to take me to their camp and there keeping me without provisions should I not provide for them more abuntantly [*sic*].[9]

Faced with such a threat, Procter decided to gamble all in one last desperate effort to open water communications with the supply base at Long Point and secure badly needed foodstuffs.

The immediate effect of Barclay's loss to Perry appears to have been negligible. Procter waited three full days (September 13) before calling a Council of War to assess the situation. At the meeting, from which Procter's second in command was deliberately excluded, it was decided to withdraw from Amherstburg.[10] Immediately after the meeting, orders were issued to the troops to begin dismantling the fortifications. When the native population witnessed the destruction of government buildings and public stores, they were furious and demanded a "talk" with Procter. On September 18, Tecumseh delivered his famous "yellow dog" speech in which he referred to Procter as a cur that runs away with its tail between its legs when frightened.[11]

After this inflammatory address the situation at Amherstburg was tense and over the next two days agents of the Indian Department worked feverishly to convince the natives that they were not being abandoned. Rather, the British were withdrawing to a more secure position from which they could resist any American attack. On September 20, Procter formally replied to Tecumseh, trying to take some of the sting out of his attack by giving assurances that he would stop at Chatham and make a stand against the enemy, vowing to mix his bones with their bones if fate so dictated.

On September 23, the remaining buildings associated with the fort were destroyed and the troops marched to Sandwich. A further four days were spent organizing the men, women, and children, collecting wagons, and preparing for the arduous march to Chatham. Thus, a total of seventeen days were taken to withdraw from the frontier. The question arises, what if Procter had waited those seventeen days for additional supplies to arrive? How might the Lake Erie battle have turned out then?

The decision to retreat to Chatham, though tactically sound, was poorly planned and lacked the drive and coordination necessary to make it a success. Valuable supplies which Procter had been pleading for the previous month were burned, thrown in the river, or simply left behind for the enemy to capture. Tired, hungry, and low in spirits, the British troops were easy prey for the advancing Americans who overtook them near Moraviantown and defeated them at the Battle of the Thames.[12]

The most immediate impact of the British loss at the Battle of Lake Erie was therefore the retreat and subsequent defeat of the Right Division at the Battle of the Thames. Some sixteen months after the Declaration of War, the American troops finally swept British forces from along the Detroit frontier. Following the battle at the Thames, Harrison ordered his troops to advance to the adjacent Moravian village and sacked the town by burning every building to deny a refuge for the survivors of the engagement. For the residents of the Western District of Upper Canada, it was but a prelude to the tide of destruction that would sweep through the area.

Upon his return to Amherstburg with some six hundred British prisoners of war, Harrison took steps to provide for the civil administration of the recently conquered territory. By proclamation dated October 18, he promised protection of private property, compensation for requisitioned supplies, and the orderly governing of the occupied territory through locally appointed officials. His declaration was similar in many respects to Brock's proclamation following the capture of Detroit in August 1812, and like Brock's declaration, proved just as difficult to uphold under the pressures of short supplies, limited manpower, and the pervasive threat of an enemy counteroffensive.[13]

Harrison also took immediate steps to provide accommodation for the detachment left behind as a guard at Amherstburg. Since the smoking ruins of Fort Amherstburg were not suitable for garrisoning his men, he ordered the immediate construction of a small stockaded work, Fort Covington, on the outskirts of town. He assured the secretary of war, John Armstrong, that "the small work at Malden [was] capable of resisting anything but a regular seige and even then it [would] not be taken without great difficulty."[14]

Harrison was also determined to reach a rapprochement with the remnants of the Indian confederacy that fought with the British. The defeat at the Thames and the death of Tecumseh seriously weakened the fighting spirit of the native groups. Harrison seized on this advantage to negotiate a "provisional Indian armistice . . . granting the Potawatomi, Wyandot, Miami, Ottawa, and Chippewa the right to occupy their normal hunting grounds until a formal peace council was convened." To insure Indian compliance with the terms of the treaty, the Americans demanded women and children as hostages as a guarantee of good behavior.[15]

The defeat on Lake Erie and the subsequent British withdrawal and defeat at Moraviantown was thus also directly responsible for neutralizing the native threat in the Old Northwest. With the death of Tecumseh and the loss of British support, native resistance to encroachments on ancestral lands collapsed and with it the dream of an Indian confederacy. With these matters settled, Harrison relinquished overall command to Brigadier General Lewis Cass and hastened to the Niagara frontier.

Responsibility for the Canadian side of the Detroit River was assigned to Captain William Puthuff who had charge of the troops stationed at Fort Covington. He was ordered to "prevent the inhabitants from holding any communication with the enemy and to afford such assistance to the police of the country as may be found necessary." Noting that in a command such as his, it was difficult to frame precise instructions, Cass cautioned Puthuff to "be vigilent [*sic*] patrolling the country, in preventing all depredations upon the property of the people and in procuring intelligence."[16]

Cass was equally concerned that appropriate steps be taken to insure the compliance of the population located inland along the River Thames (or Trench as the Americans referred to it) and the scattered settlements clustered about the various area milling establishments. He ordered Lieutenant Larwill with a detachment of some forty men of the 27th Infantry Regiment to journey to the River Trench area with four specific objectives: to restore order and quiet to the people of the country; to prevent all communication with the enemy; to ascertain the situation, prospects, and objects of the enemy; and to aid the commissary in procuring wheat, grinding it into flour, and transporting it back to Malden.[17]

On the evening of December 5, Larwill and his party were surprised and captured by a smaller party of Canadian militia, under Lieutenant H. Medcalf, 2d Norfolk Militia, after offering only a "feeble resistance."[18] When Cass learned of his defeat, he ordered out a much stronger party of some 250 rangers to go in pursuit of the Canadian militia but they were unsuccessful in catching them. The capture of Larwill's party was a timely reminder that American influence was limited to those areas falling within the military umbrella of Amherstburg and that the position on the Canadian side of the Detroit River was far from secure.

Cass and later commanders with responsibility for the Detroit frontier were keenly aware how tentative their hold was on the Canadian side of the river. Fort Shelby at Detroit and the surrounding posts were at the end of a long supply line stretching south into Ohio and Kentucky. As a result, the posts were chronically understaffed and often lacked essential supplies. Complaints from district commanders are reminiscent of Procter's frequent appeals to his supply center for additional support.

There were other parallels between the period of British occupation of Detroit and the American occupation of Amherstburg. The extensive buffer zone extending east from the Detroit River remained, as had Procter's buffer in Michigan and Ohio, in a state of constant flux, shifting back and forth depending on the ability of one side or the other to harass scouting and foraging parties. Just as Procter had continually probed at American counteroffensives to disrupt the troops and deflect an all-out attack while at the same time securing badly needed supplies, so too Lewis Cass and his successors had to contend with a hostile population, well supplied with corn and cattle and ever willing to provide aid and comfort to the enemy. As Procter's situation became more critical, the measures he adopted with respect to the local population became increasingly harsh. American officers commanding the recently conquered territory in Upper Canada found themselves in a similar situation and responded with equally rigorous measures.

Perhaps the single difference between the British and American commanders and their situations was the extensive use of native warriors by the British. Outmanned as they were, the British necessarily grasped at all available resources in their struggle to preserve a distinctive national entity in North America based on a different social and political order. The willingness of native groups to participate with the British rested in no small degree on the unceasing pressure by American frontier settlements to divest Indians of their ancestral lands.

Having stated that, it should be noted that American military commanders were not unwilling to deploy whatever means were available to them to achieve their objectives. Foraging parties that operated throughout the Western District employed an extensive network of spies recruited from among former residents of Upper Canada. During the summer of 1814, Lieutenant Colonel George Croghan of the 2d Rifle Regiment, the commanding officer at Detroit, organized a company of Canadian scouts to undertake raids deep into the heart of enemy territory. These men waged their own war of attrition by looting and burning homes and mills of area residents. As one American officer, Captain L. McCormick, who commanded the rangers, complained, these "volunteers [are] a set of the most unprincipled rascals . . . bent on loot." One party of such raiders was captured during the winter of 1813–14 and subsequently tried at Ancaster. Eight were later hanged but were spared being drawn and quartered, the punishment usually reserved for convicted traitors.[19]

Through the winter of 1813–14, American officials became increasingly alarmed over reports of a possible British counteroffensive to recapture the thinly defended Detroit frontier; these fears were not without foundation. Sir Gordon Drummond, commander of the forces in Upper Canada, had urged on his superior a quick winter strike against Amherstburg by regulars and militia moving in sleighs down the frozen Thames River. The lack of sufficient snow and mild winter weather forced cancellation of the plan.[20] This renewal of military activity by the British caused considerable unease among those American officers charged with holding the buffer territory.

The threat of a British attack, the hostility of the local population, and the continuous sniping at patrols by roving Indian bands exacerbated an already difficult situation. In the early months of 1814, the commanding officer at Amherstburg, Major W. H. Puthuff, had less than a hundred effective troops composed of regulars from the 17th, 19th, 26th, 27th, and 28th Regiments of Infantry.[21] Without an adequate military presence, he warned he could not guarantee the full cooperation of the local populace. By April the situation had not improved. Captain J. Belt, 28th Infantry in command at Fort Covington, reported that he had seven Michigan cavalry, forty-three Rangers, thirty-two rank and file of the 24th Regiment, and seventy men of the 28th, although nearly a third of these men were sick or otherwise employed.[22]

Moreover, with two major campaigns planned for 1814, one on the Niagara frontier to wrest control of Fort George and Niagara from the British and the other against Mackinac in the far northwest, there were precious few soldiers left to meet the needs of the garrisons at Malden, Sandwich, and Detroit. Senior officials at Washington, however, were reluctant to acknowledge the need for additional troops at such posts as Fort Covington. Secretary of War John Armstrong dismissed McArthur's concerns by reminding him:

> the Danger with respect to Detroit can, under present circumstances arise only from Indians. . . . The British troops . . . have ample occupation in defending their posts on the Niagara River. What under these circumstances have we to fear at Detroit. An Indian attack! . . . Is it not more probable that the savages will be called and concentrated for the defence of Mackinaw? There are a set of alarmists who, from a different set of motives, labour to keep the public in a state of fever.[23]

In words which echoed similar statements by Prevost to Procter, Armstrong was suggesting to McArthur he would have to make do with what he had.

Not only were the quantity of troops a problem, the quality of both officers and men also proved troublesome to McArthur. Though generally commanded by regular officers drawn from the 8th Military District, much of the American force stationed along the Detroit River was composed of locally raised militia units, rangers, and turncoat Canadians. In the spring of 1814, Lieutenant Colonel Croghan was in charge of Detroit and surrounding posts. On his own initiative, he commenced construction of a post near Lake St. Clair, later named Fort Gratiot.[24] With his departure for Fort Shelby, he placed Major Rawlins in command. However, within days of his departure, Rawlins took offense at Croghan's action and refused the command. Croghan ordered him placed under arrest and transferred command to Captain A. Gray of the 24th Regiment. Captain Gray was soon embroiled in a local controversy regarding a shopkeeper at Malden and was himself placed under arrest. With two of the senior officers at Detroit under arrest, McArthur was faced with a serious problem in leadership and temporarily suspended charges against Gray. Nor were the regular soldiers immune from the necessity of disciplinary action. A private stationed at Amherstburg, Hyatt Leasure, was brought before a court-martial, convicted of desertion, and ordered shot.[25]

A lack of good officers was compounded by the recurring difficulty of obtaining adequate supplies. In May 1814, Croghan spoke forcefully about the problems faced by the Quartermaster General's department. In a dispatch to McArthur he noted that the department was

> too poorly equipped with funds to answer the many large demands which are hourly brought against it. Captain McClosky at my request drew on the government for $20,000. When it is recollected that the Quartermaster has to furnish everything at this place—provisions, fuel, transportation, labourers and the like, it will appear that this sum although large cannot serve us long. Our salt provision is entirely exhausted. . . . I am still issuing rations of flour to the poor inhabitants of this territory. . . . Provisions are not to be purchased here at any price.[26]

Thus, supply problems along the Detroit were not unique to Henry Procter and the British Right Division.

Like the British before them, the American occupation force stepped up the pressure on the resident population to help alleviate serious food shortages and deny enemy troops any material advantage in this region. The civilians living in the Western District suffered the most from this policy, losing not only their livestock and grain crops but also the mills used to grind wheat into life-sustaining flour. For example, in February 1814, Major Smiley led a detachment of some two hundred mounted Michigan militia on a foraging expedition to the River Thames district. They seized one thousand bushels of grain and commandeered sleighs and wagons to transport their prize back to Malden.[27] Three months later, Croghan informed McArthur of further raids to this area. "I have ascertained that the enemy has a large store of flour near the grande River under the guard of a Sergeant and squad. I shall capture the guard and destroy the flour. My spies went out about 6 days ago. They have orders to dismantle Talbots mills and destroy all large stores of grain or corn on their route."[28] Supply problems were thus not unique to the British while Procter was in charge of the right wing posted along the Detroit frontier.

In order to support his troops operating in this area, Croghan recommended establishing a small outpost along the Thames. McArthur, as the commander responsible for the 8th Military District which included the Canadian territory east of the Detroit River, was concerned with the dispersal of troops initiated by Croghan and decided to visit the district in the summer of 1814 to determine for himself what was needed. After surveying the situation, he decided against building a post along the Thames River. As he noted in his dispatch to Armstrong, "it would not be within supporting distance of Detroit. . . . I have ever been more in favour of consolidating than dividing our force."[29] Instead, he recommended construction of a substantial fortification at Amherstburg. With the uncertainty of the fighting in the Niagara theater and the planned assault on Mackinac Island, McArthur was anxious to maintain control over the vital shipping lane along the Detroit River. As he observed in instructions issued to Croghan, "Were the enemy to again possess himself of the strait, he would at once cut off all communication by water between Lake Erie and Detroit."[30]

Having committed himself to a strong presence at Malden, McArthur issued orders for the new resident commanding officer, Colonel John Miller of the 17th Regiment, to begin construction of a field work on the ruins of the old British fort. Ordnance, tools, and a reinforcement of manpower were dispatched to Amherstburg in the summer of 1814 to carry out this work. However, progress was slow. By mid-September Miller had to report that "the work at this post progresses but slowly for want of hands. . . . Out of 700 men there are about 340 reported present and fit for duty, the balance are either sick, on command, or on Extra Duty."[31] Shortages continued to hinder completion of the fort.

At the end of September, Miller was transferred with his regiment to Fort Erie, leaving barely twenty effective men at Malden![32] Miller's replacement, Captain Charles Gratiot, one of four French youths appointed by Jefferson to West Point after the Louisiana purchase, was dismayed by the situation at Malden. Although some additional manpower was received, hard currency was still in short supply. He informed McArthur, "Mr. Lafrelle[?] of the River Raison [*sic*] contracted to furnish this Post with Plank for our Batteries. . . . It will be out of his power to carry on his engagement any further if he is not shortly furnished with funds.[33]

Finding quarters and rations for these additional troops while the new post was under construction added to the problems which Miller and later Gratiot had to face. Every expediency was used to provide for the comfort of the men. Numerous private residences vacated by the local militiamen were seized and occupied by American troops. The residence of Matthew Elliott, former superintendent of the Indian Department, sustained extensive damage during the period it was occupied. His widow subsequently applied for compensation to render the building habitable. Similarly, the gracious Georgian residence of William Mills was severely damaged while occupied by American regulars and required extensive repairs. In other cases, buildings were moved from the town to within the confines of the new fort. A log building which formerly served as a schoolhouse was relocated to the fort. Under Miller's orders cattle, wheat, fruit, vegetables, and whiskey were seized from private citizens and given to the troops. As the harvest season approached Miller took even sterner measures. By proclamation dated September 1814, the citizens of the occupied district were ordered to deliver over "all the Flour, Wheat, & Oats which they may have on hand, more than is necessary for the use and consumption of their families and stock . . . persons withholding such surplus shall be severely punished." The proclamation also provided for a fixed schedule of payment for the seized produce and appointment of three persons to determine if surplus grain was being held back. To provide the local commander with the necessary power to implement such measures, civilian administration was abolished and martial law put in its place.[34]

Despite the promises of payment, the citizens of Amherstburg and the surrounding area were deprived of their private property without compensation. In all, residents of the Western District claimed over £50,000 worth of damages suffered in loss of food, clothing, and property at the hands of the Americans.[35] These injustices were forcefully presented directly to McArthur in a petition signed by the leading citizens of the town:

> We are sorry sir to inform you that since the issuing of the proclamation by General Harrison by which we were promised protection to our persons and property, property has been taken from individuals.

> . . . The sufferers in general have not received any remuneration whatever to the great injury and distress of many of them. . . . In the impressment of horses . . . the greatest abuses have taken place. . . . We lament to inform you that the most arbitrary, degrading, and ignominious punishments have been inflicted with impunity on several of the inhabitants of this District without the form of trial or least colour of justice.[36]

The harsh treatment handed out to the local residents was duplicated when dealing with the residents along the River Thames. Although the intention was to purchase, foraging patrols often ended up being nothing more than pillaging expeditions.

By September 1814, the campaign against the Western District had been intensified. In a dispatch of September 4, Governor Cass remarked that

> the supplies of wheat upon the River Trenche [Thames] are most abundant and in the event of the enemy advancing into this quarter, they would find it of vital importance to their operations. They appear already to appreciate its value, as two of their agents were taken a few days since, who were making contracts with the people for the delivery of their wheat. We cannot procure it, for it is too far from this post and any detachment sent into that quarter would be liable to be cut off. My opinion is that all this grain should be destroyed, and I am by no means convinced it would not be sound policy to break up the settlements below this post. . . . it appears a harsh and rigorous step, but it is certainly no time for weak, timid and irresolute measures.[37]

McArthur concurred with the governor's assessment. At the end of October, he set out with approximately eight hundred men ostensibly with the purpose of striking at the British base at Burlington Heights. However, a local Canadian militia officer was not convinced that Burlington was the objective. Captain John Bostwick of the Norfolk militia observed, "I cannot think their intentions are of that nature but rather that they intend ravaging this district. They are composed almost entirely of Kentuckians and undisciplined."[38]

Bostwick's fears were not without foundation. The American military commander had even more draconian measures under active consideration. During the winter of 1814–15 McArthur seriously contemplated a "scorched earth policy" to deny the enemy reason for returning to the district. As he informed Secretary of War James Monroe, "would it not be well to send a force into Canada next summer which would lay it waste and in this way interpose between us and the enemy a desert which he could not easily pass." Colonel Anthony Butler, the officer commanding at Amherstburg, picked up on this idea. He informed McArthur that he planned to follow a "pretty strict regime for the River Trench and the New Settlement population; a little blood letting may do them good and make the country tranquil; yet I am of the opinion decidedly that the safest course is to depopulate the territory."[39] Only the formal ratification of the terms of peace negotiated at Ghent in December 1814 put an end to hostilities and spared the residents of the Western District further hardships under the American occupation.

In assessing the overall effect of the defeat on Lake Erie for the British war effort, the evidence suggests that it was negligible. Though the British conducted periodic raids against marauding parties of enemy troops scouting the Western District, they made no concerted effort to regain the captured territory after the abortive plan of a dash against the frontier in January 1814. Harsh though the reality was to the local residents, the capture and occupation of the region along the Detroit River did not hamper the principal objective of the war which was to preserve a stronghold in North America. Indeed, the British still managed to send supplies to the upper lakes posts via the land route leading to Georgian Bay.

The most critical impact of the loss of the fleet and withdrawal from the frontier was thus the abandonment of the Western District to an enemy occupying force for the duration of the war. For the native people who relied on British support, the loss was crushing and extinguished all hope of resistance to American advances. The Battle of Lake Erie was of local importance and its effects largely limited to the immediate Detroit theater of the conflict. Here the impact was severe, as the residents experienced personal hardship at the hands of the occupying American force. In this, they shared a similar fate with their neighbors across the river who had endured equal hardships in the early stages of the war when the British had been in control of the region. Such was the legacy of war along the Detroit frontier.

R. DAVID EDMUNDS

Tecumseh's Native Allies: Warriors Who Fought for the Crown

The decade and a half following the Treaty of Greenville was a trying time for the Indian people of the Old Northwest. Although the treaty, signed in 1795, had ostensibly established boundaries between Indian and white lands in Ohio and Indiana, these lines of demarcation were honored more in their violation than in their compliance. Eager for additional farmlands, American squatters crossed the treaty lines to clear fields and build cabins in regions that had been guaranteed to the tribesmen. Meanwhile, white hunters from Kentucky ranged as far north as the Wabash and Illinois, and in 1801 even William Henry Harrison, the governor of Indiana Territory, admitted that:

> The people of Kentucky . . . make a constant practice of crossing over the Indians lands opposite to them every fall to kill deer, bear, and buffalo—the latter from being in great abundance a few years ago is now scarcely to be met with. One white hunter will destroy more game than five of the common Indians—the latter generally contenting himself with a sufficiency for present subsistence—while the other eager after game hunt for the skin of the animal alone.[1]

In addition, the account books of Indian traders in the region illustrate that the fur trade also was declining. Shawnee and Miami warriors still ran their trap lines, but they now found many of their traps to be empty. Once a self-sufficient people, the tribesmen faced economic deprivation. They no longer had sufficient food for their cooking pots, and they could not afford to buy those trade items which once had been luxuries, but now were necessities.[2]

In response, some of the tribesmen began to sell that commodity which they still possessed, but which the Long Knives coveted so dearly: their land. During the first decade of the nineteenth century, Harrison and other federal officials continued to chip away at the remaining Indian land base, purchasing vast acreages of the Mississippi and Ohio valleys in a series of piecemeal treaties through which the government of the United States acquired over 35 million acres of Indian land. Many of these sales were lubricated with frontier whiskey, and most of the tracts were purchased from chiefs friendly to the federal government, but once the ink had dried on the documents the land was irretrievably lost to the Indians. Of course, in exchange, the tribesmen received their usual quota of trade goods and annuities, but their shrinking land base only accelerated their economic deterioration.[3]

Hoping to stem this decline, some tribesmen attempted to walk the white man's road. Moravian and Quaker missionaries had long been active among the Delawares in Ohio and Indiana, and in the years following the Treaty of Greenville their efforts accelerated. Spurred on by the passage of the Indian Intercourse Acts and the Jefferson administration's promotion of agricultural programs, both religious personnel and Indian agents established "model farms" or "agricultural stations" and endeavored to transform the Indians of the Old Northwest into small yeoman farmers.[4]

At first they seemed successful. By 1805 several villages of Moravian Delawares were attempting to farm along the White River in Indiana, and several influential village chiefs also gave at least lip service to the government's programs. Among the Wyandots, prominent leaders such as Tarhe (the Crane), or Walk-in-the-Water supported the government programs, while at Fort Wayne, Five Medals, a Potawatomi chief, and Little Turtle, the most influential spokesman for the Miamis, also cooperated with Indian Agent William Wells. In Ohio, the aging Shawnee patriarch, Black Hoof, endorsed a Quaker mission at Wapakoneta; and along the lower Wabash, other village chiefs also fell prey to the government's promises. In return, federal officials funneled presents and annuity payments through these "medal chiefs," further increasing their influence and transforming them into the cornucopia through which the government's largess was delivered. In addition, these and other influential Indian leaders were invited to Washington, where they were "wined and dined" and shown the power and majesty of their Great Father. Although these pilgrimages seemed to be much more effective in reaffirming the loyalty of friendly chiefs than in winning the support of recalcitrants, Indians from both camps obviously enjoyed the excursions.[5]

But not all the tribesmen subscribed to these efforts. Considerable numbers of Wyandots, Shawnees, Potawatomis, and more western tribesmen still preferred the ways of their fathers, and they clung tenaciously to the hope that somehow those days would be rekindled. Although even the American government's "medal chiefs" periodically visited Amherstburg, it was these more traditional tribesmen who maintained their ties to the Crown. Many met regularly with British agents, and although members of the British Indian Department such as Matthew Elliott and Alexander McKee no longer were welcome south of the lakes, the Crown's influence still permeated many of the tribes of Michigan and Wisconsin. Ostensibly serving as traders, mixed-blood merchants such as Isadore Chaine or Billy Caldwell still worked in the Crown's behalf, assuring their kinsmen that their British father had not forgotten his children and still worked for their benefit.[6]

Yet even the more traditional warriors' ties to the Crown were rather tenuous. In the decade following the American Revolution, British agents functioning on the local level often had made promises which the Crown had not fulfilled. Since agents such as Elliott and McKee also were traders who had married into the tribes, it is not surprising that they overstated the British commitment, but in 1794, when John Graves Simcoe, the governor of Upper Canada, met with the tribes on the Sandusky River in Ohio, the Indians interpreted the meeting as indicative of considerable British support. Of course the subsequent construction of Fort Miamis, near modern Toledo, Ohio, only confirmed their faith that their British father did indeed intend to assist his Indian children.[7]

In the following year that faith was shattered. On August 20, 1794, after retreating before the Americans at Fallen Timbers, the multitribal army assembled along the Maumee confidently expected to regroup at Fort Miamis, and with the assistance of the British garrison turn the tide against the Long Knives. But when they reached the fort, they found that Major William Campbell, the commander of the post, would not admit them inside the palisade. Dumbfounded, the Indians were forced to flee toward Lake Erie as Anthony Wayne's army destroyed their villages. It is not surprising that on September 10, 1813, almost two decades later, when another British military commander, Major-General Henry Procter, decided to abandon Fort Malden, Tecumseh reminded him that "when we retreated to our father's fort at that place [Fort Miamis], the gates were shut against us. . . . We are afraid that our father will do so again at this time."[8]

The Indians, therefore, still welcomed British assistance, but they were not so naive as to believe that it would be delivered free of charge. They still met with British agents at Amherstburg, thanking them for their gifts of lead and gunpowder, but the Indians were not the catspaws of British Indian policy as the Americans charged. More accurately, they were independent people who were acting in what they perceived to be their own interests. Most realized that they held certain similarities of interests with the British; when those interests coalesced, they were willing to join the British as allies. But by 1812 almost all the Indians were fighting for the Indians, not for the Crown.

Indeed, the Indian resistance which emerged in the Old Northwest prior to the War of 1812 at first surprised the British as much as it did the Americans. Neither side ever understood the origins of the movement, for its inception was steeped more thoroughly in religion than in political or military affairs.[9]

Traditionally, during times of great social and economic stress, Indian people have turned to their manitous for deliverance. And for the tribes of the Old Northwest, the decade following the Treaty of Greenville was a catastrophic period. Not only did their economic base deteriorate, they were debilitated by alcohol and subjected to a series of epidemics that contributed to demographic losses during these years. In addition, they suffered markedly at the hands of the American judicial system. White frontiersmen accused of crimes against the tribes rarely were convicted, for as Harrison admitted, "a great many of the Inhabitants of the Frontier consider the murdering of the Indians in the highest degree meritorious." Overwhelmed by such problems, Indian society came apart. Once peaceful villages became the scenes of drunken desperation, and the kinship system, the very warp of tribal fabric, no longer could maintain itself.[10]

In April 1805, an alcoholic Shawnee medicine man experienced the first of a series of visions which profoundly changed many Indians' lives. Known as Lalawethika, or the "Noise Maker," the Shawnee claimed that he had died or ascended to the firmament where the Master of Life first showed him both heaven and hell, then provided him with a new religious doctrine for all the tribes. Assuming a new name, Tenskwatawa, or the "Open Door," he began to promulgate his faith to the Shawnees and to neighboring tribes, where his doctrines found many adherents.[11]

According to the Shawnee Prophet, the Indians (and even the British and French) had been created by the Master of Life, but the Americans were the children of the Great Serpent, the epitome of evil in the world.

Before the Americans had arrived, the Indians' world had been orderly and they had been the masters of their homeland, but the Americans had spread their evil and now the Indians' very existence was threatened. In response, the tribesmen should renounce American technology and return to the ways of their fathers. They could still use firearms to defend themselves, but they should hunt with bows and arrows. They also should relinquish white clothing, liquor, foods, and economic activities. The Prophet also offered new rituals and ceremonies which would revitalize the tribes, and he promised to create a new Indian Eden. Especially suspect were those Indians who had acculturated and had adopted American ways, for such behavior meant that they too were servants of the Great Serpent and were guilty of witchcraft.[12]

Not surprisingly, such accusations threatened the American medal chiefs and those Indians who had settled at the Quaker or Moravian mission stations. In the spring of 1806, after some of the Prophet's adherents burned several Moravian Delawares, the medal chiefs and their missionary allies complained to federal officials. In response, Harrison condemned the Shawnee holy man and wrote to the Delawares, charging:

> My heart is filled with grief, and my eyes are dissolved in tears, at the news which has reached me. You have been celebrated for your wisdom above all the tribes of red people. . . . If he is really a prophet, ask of him to cause the sun to stand still—the moon to alter its course—the rivers to cease to flow—the dead to rise from their graves. If he does these things, you may then believe that he has been sent from God.[13]

Harrison either overlooked or was ignorant of a forthcoming eclipse, but not so the Prophet. Answering Harrison's challenge, Tenskwatawa promised that he would cause the sun to die, then resurrect it; and on June 16, 1806, when an almost complete eclipse of the sun took place across Ohio and Indiana, the Prophet's stock accelerated. Even tribesmen who had remained skeptical of his sincerity now became converts.[14]

During the next year Indians from the Great Lakes to the Gulf of Mexico made pilgrimages to his village. This influx of Indians frightened both American officials and frontiersmen and caused such food shortages in the Prophet's camp that in the spring of 1808 he moved from Ohio to establish a new village, Prophetstown, at the juncture of the Tippecanoe and Wabash rivers in western Indiana.[15]

Tecumseh played only a minor role in these affairs. An older brother of the Prophet, Tecumseh had emerged as a prominent young Shawnee war chief and served as the village chief in the village where Tenskwatawa initially experienced his visions, but at first he did not participate in the spread of the new faith and remained entirely in the Prophet's shadow. Tecumseh did meet with officials in Ohio during 1807, but he exercised only minimal influence, and he is not mentioned in any documents from that period. Indeed, although the correspondence of contemporary British and American officials is replete with references to Tenskwatawa, they make no reference to Tecumseh until the summer of 1808, when William Claus wrote in his diary that "the Prophet's brother" had visited Amherstburg. The Shawnee war chief is not listed in American accounts until 1810, when Harrison commented that Tecumseh had emerged as "really the efficient man . . . the Moses of the family . . . daring in the extreme, and capable of any undertaking." Obviously then, Tenskwatawa's religious promises, not Tecumseh's plans for political and military unity, were the catalyst which first attracted the warriors to Ohio. Tecumseh used his brother's religious movement as the base for his efforts to unite the tribes, but this transformation was slow to emerge, and Tecumseh did not transcend his brother until late 1810 or 1811.[16]

Why then have historians traditionally argued that the Indian resistance emerged around Tecumseh's efforts for a political and military alliance? The answer lies in the ethnocentric bias of Tecumseh's Anglo and American contemporaries, and in the perspective of white historians. They championed Tecumseh as the author of the Indian movement, for the Shawnee war chief's solution to the Indian dilemma seemed quite logical to them. Tecumseh did what they would have done: he attempted to unify the tribes politically. Such a solution was alien to most Indians (and was adamantly opposed by the government's medal chiefs) but it seemed eminently logical to Europeans and Americans. Unlike the Prophet's religious revitalization movement, which was more traditionally "Indian" in its response, Tecumseh's endeavors appealed to both the British and the Americans. Surely, therefore, the Shawnee war chief was the primary instigator of the Indian resistance and his charlatan brother had only limited, if bizarre, influence! Of course, such an assumption was not shared by the Indians, but until recently it has been promulgated in most textbooks.[17]

But if the Prophet or Tecumseh attracted warriors to the Indian, and secondarily to the British, cause, who were they? Obviously, most were cultural traditionalists who had little interest in the federal government's acculturation programs. Many were younger warriors, still eager to "earn their stripes" in the accepted manner of their fathers, but others were older men who opposed the changes swirling around them. Many were described as pro-British by American Indian agents, but such accusations probably marked the failure of these agents to enlist them into the government's acculturation programs. Yet, in retrospect, most were fighting for an Indian cause, more than for the Crown.

And that cause had many facets. Certainly some of the warriors who fought with Tecumseh shared his hopes for Indian unity, but others seemed eager to join in the hostilities not through any devotion to Tecumseh's goals, but as an opportunity to enhance their own personal stature and to strike back at the Americans. Foremost among this group was a war chief whom Indian Agent William Wells described as "the greatest warrior in the west . . . the pivot on which the minds of all the Western Indians turned. . . . [He] has more influence than any other Indian": Main Poc of the Potawatomis. Particularly influential among the Potawatomis, Kickapoos, and the Sacs and Foxes, Main Poc's usual residence was a village at the juncture of Rock Creek and the Kankakee River in northeastern Illinois. Main Poc had been born with no fingers or thumb on his left hand, and he claimed that the deformity was a special sign that he had been blessed by the manitous and so he became a wabeno, or medicine man. He rose to prominence through his campaigns against the Osages, and by 1812 he was about fifty years old.[18]

If Tecumseh epitomized most American's conception of the "noble savage," Main Poc undoubtedly personified the opposite end of the spectrum. Addicted to alcohol, the old Potawatomi was a notorious lecher with a violent temper who lashed out at both friends and foes alike. When going to war he often wore a sash of human scalps tied around his waist, with strings of "bear claws, and the bills of hawks and owls tied round his ankles." Attempting to impress Main Poc with the power of the federal government, officials in 1808 had conducted him to Washington where he met with Jefferson, but while other Indians on the tour visited sites around the capital, the Potawatomi remained in his room drinking and threatening the chamber maids.[19] He refused to meet with a delegation of Quakers; and on his return trip to the west, he became so intoxicated that he attempted to murder his wife, who had accompanied him on the journey. He refused Tecumseh's pleas for intertribal unity and his continued attacks upon the Osages did much to keep them from joining the Shawnee's confederacy. Moreover, raids by his warriors upon southern Illinois during the summer of 1811 also contradicted Tecumseh's orders and prompted Harrison to march against Prophetstown.[20]

Main Poc did not participate in the Battle of Tippecanoe, but in 1811 he moved his village to the Huron River, south of Detroit. There he was joined by bands of Potawatomis and Kickapoos, and in early June 1812, when news of the declaration of war reached the region, he crossed the river to Amherstburg. He was active in the skirmishing along the Canard River, and on July 19 he received a minor yet painful gunshot wound to his neck. After the skirmish, he actually scalped the body of a British soldier, but when he displayed the bright red scalp back at Malden, the fallen soldier's comrades denounced him as a coward and he lost considerable influence. Three weeks later he also participated in the Battle of Monguagon, and when the fighting ended, he tomahawked and scalped one of the hapless American prisoners.[21]

Although he remained in Canada, he dispatched messengers to his kinsmen encouraging them to assault Fort Dearborn; and on August 15, 1812, when the garrison attempted to evacuate that fort, they were ambushed by a large war party at least partially comprised of his followers. One of the leaders in the assault was Mad Sturgeon, Main Poc's brother-in-law. Meanwhile, the Potawatomi wabeno assisted Tecumseh and Brock in the capture of Detroit, then accompanied Muir's ill-fated expedition toward Fort Wayne. Although Muir wisely retreated before Harrison's oncoming army, Main Poc informed the British commander that he had experienced a vision and the British and Indians should stand and fight. Muir wisely declined.[22]

Main Poc spent the winter of 1812–13 back in Illinois recruiting additional followers among the Sacs, Potawatomis, and Winnebagos, but in the spring he returned to Canada. Although contemporary accounts do not specifically mention his participation in the campaigns against Fort Meigs, he probably was in attendance. The slaughter of American prisoners after Dudley's Defeat in May 1813 was precipitated by some unruly Potawatomis, and the action smacks suspiciously of Main Poc's handiwork. Motivated more by personal interests than by any loyalty to Tecumseh or the Crown, Main Poc led a large party of followers back into Michigan in August 1813, when Tecumseh and Procter retreated toward the Thames, to await the outcome of the upcoming battle in Canada. If his former allies won, he planned to fall upon the retreating Americans, but if Harrison's forces were successful, he intended to flee westward across Michigan.[23]

The Battle of the Thames was an American victory and Main Poc fled to the St. Joseph River in western Michigan where he unsuccessfully tried to rally the remnants of Tecumseh's confederacy. Although he raided a few settlements along the Wabash, his efforts were ineffectual and his influence declined. In 1815, after learning of the Treaty of Ghent, he traveled to Mackinac where British officials confirmed that the peace treaty had been signed. Embittered, he refused to participate in the negotiations between the Indians and the United States, and retreated to a new camp near Manistee, on the eastern shores of Lake Michigan. Debilitated by alcohol and now grown deaf, the old wabeno died in the spring of 1816.[24]

If Main Poc's association with Tecumseh was tenuous, Roundhead, a Wyandot chief originally from the Sandusky River, was a devoted follower of the Shawnee war chief. Originally a convert to the Prophet's teachings, Roundhead brought many of his followers to Greenville, Ohio, in May 1807, where they settled in the Prophet's village. In September of that year he accompanied Tecumseh, Blue Jacket, and several other Indians from Greenville to Chillicothe, where they met with Governor Thomas Kirker. In 1808 he followed the Shawnee brothers to Prophetstown, their new village on the Wabash, but whether he fought in the Battle of Tippecanoe in November 1811 remains unknown. By the summer of 1812 he had relocated at Brownstown, the Wyandot settlement across from Amherstburg, where he attempted to persuade his kinsmen, led by Walk-in-the-Water, to join with Tecumseh. Roundhead probably participated in the battles of Brownstown and Monguagon, and in August he assisted in the capture of Detroit; following Hull's surrender, Tecumseh gave him a scarlet sash which previously had been awarded to the Shawnee by General Isaac Brock.[25]

In September he accompanied Tecumseh and Major Adam Muir on the latter's ill-fated expedition to assist the Potawatomis in their unsuccessful siege of Fort Wayne, and after the British retreat he spent the autumn of 1812 at Brownstown. By 1813 Procter considered Roundhead to be second only in influence to Tecumseh, and in January the Wyandot commanded the Indian warriors who joined with the British to defeat the Americans at Frenchtown. In the aftermath of the battle, Roundhead made General James Winchester his personal prisoner, but he lacked either the influence or the inclination to prevent the subsequent slaughter of the American prisoners.[26]

In April 1813, Roundhead led part of the Indian forces who accompanied Procter at the siege of Fort Meigs, and although most of the warriors became impatient with the siege and abandoned the British effort, Roundhead remained in Ohio until Procter retreated. In August 1813, when pro-American Wyandots attempted to undermine British influence at Brownstown, Roundhead—ever loyal to the Crown—chastised them for supporting the Americans and advised them to remain neutral. According to Roundhead, the pro-British Indians welcomed the forthcoming American invasion and were "happy to learn that your Father [Harrison] is coming out of his hole, as he has been like a ground hog under the ground and will save us much trouble in walking to meet him." Unfortunately, however, Roundhead was killed or died of natural causes shortly after the council, and Procter admitted that "the Indian cause and ours experienced a serious loss" in his passing.[27]

Although other Wyandot leaders also fought for the Crown, their dedication to the British and/or Indian cause was much less devoted. Split Log, another Wyandot chief, also assisted Tecumseh and Roundhead at the capture of Detroit, and he accompanied Muir's expedition on its trek to Ohio. He also fought in the Battle of the Thames, but in 1814 he wavered between the British and American causes, first flirting with the Long Knives, then leading a force of warriors who defeated Brigadier General Duncan McArthur's expedition on the Grand River in October.[28]

Still less devoted was Walk-in-the-Water, the leader of the Wyandot village at Brownstown. Unwilling to commit himself until he was sure which side had the upper hand, Walk-in-the-Water adopted a neutral stance throughout 1811, conferring with British officials at Amherstburg, but also assuring American Indian agents that they could count upon his friendship. In July 1812, after news of the declaration of war reached the Detroit region, the Wyandot leader met repeatedly with Tecumseh, Roundhead, and even Main Poc. Impressed by the large numbers of pro-British Indians assembling at Amherstburg, he brought some of his followers over into Ontario in early July where they enjoyed the Indian Department's largess until Hull's invasion of Canada seemed to indicate that the Americans had the initiative. Responding to the American advance, Walk-in-the-Water and his followers promptly retreated back to Brownstown where they remained until news reached the Detroit region that British and Indian forces had captured the American post at Mackinac. Then, on August 2, 1812, Walk-in-the-Water led his warriors back across the Detroit River to Amherstburg.[29]

His subsequent participation in the capture of Detroit and the campaigns in Ohio remains unknown, which is probably indicative of his contribution to these ventures, but when the tide of battle turned in the Americans' favor, Walk-in-the-Water again straddled the political fence. In August 1813, he allowed pro-American Wyandots from the Sandusky region to meet with British-allied warriors at his village, but when Tecumseh, Roundhead, and British Indian agents attended the conference, he openly espoused the Crown. After Tecumseh and his retinue departed, however, Walk-in-the-Water met secretly with the pro-American Wyandots and assured them that if Harrison and a large army advanced north along the western shore of Lake Erie, he would seize strategic locations and hold them for the Long Knives. Although he again failed to honor his promise and at first retreated with British and Indian forces toward York, he refused to participate in the fighting and abandoned Tecumseh on October 4, 1813. He survived the war and died peacefully in his sleep at a village on the Huron River in 1818.[30]

Many of the other warriors survived the war. Nuscotnoemeg, or Mad Sturgeon, a Potawatomi chief from the Kankakee River in Illinois, was at Tecumseh's side when the Shawnee was killed at the Battle of the Thames, but he was spared and served his people in the postwar period. A brother-in-law to the notorious Main Poc, Mad Sturgeon also had participated in the raids against the Osages; but in the summer of 1812, when Main Poc joined the British at Detroit, Mad Sturgeon remained in the Chicago region. Assisted by Siggenauk, or Blackbird, Mad Sturgeon led the attack upon the hapless Fort Dearborn garrison, and he was wounded in the subsequent battle. In the spring of 1813 he led his followers to Amherstburg where he evidently fought in the futile attempts to capture American posts in Ohio. Following the Battle of the Thames, he retreated into northern Indiana where he continued to fight against the Americans. Convinced that further resistance was futile, he surrendered to American Indian Agent Benjamin Stickney in May 1815, at Fort Wayne. He signed the Treaty of Spring Wells (August 22, 1815), and continued to serve as a village chief until at least 1818, when his signature appears on the Treaty of St. Mary's, which ceded Potawatomi lands in western Indiana.[31]

Many other warriors fought against the Americans during the conflict. Siggenauk, a mixed-blood of Potawatomi-Ottawa descent, assisted Mad Sturgeon in the attack near Fort Dearborn. He had inherited his name from his father, also a leader from the Milwaukee region. Yet, unlike his father who was friendly to the Americans, the younger Siggenauk refused American overtures; and although he visited Washington during 1808, he remained loyal to the Crown.[32] Also loyal to the British cause was Billy Caldwell, a mixed-blood of Mohawk descent who rose to prominence among the Potawatomi community near Chicago. A son of Colonel William Caldwell, Billy had served as an Indian trader prior to the war, and he used his influence to intercede on behalf of several of the prisoners after the attack upon the Fort Dearborn garrison. He also assisted British forces at the Battle of Frenchtown, participated in the campaigns against Forts Meigs and Stephenson, and fought at Moraviantown and on the Niagara frontier. Following the death of Matthew Elliott in 1814, Caldwell was appointed assistant deputy superintendent for the Western District, a post he held until 1816. After the war he resettled at Chicago where he became the most prominent leader of the combined community of Potawatomis, Ottawas, and Chippewas living near the southern tip of Lake Michigan. He served as a justice of the peace at Chicago, assisted the Americans during the Black Hawk War, and eventually negotiated the land cessions and treaties that facilitated the removal of his people to Iowa. He died at modern Council Bluffs in 1841.[33]

Among the other Indians prominent on the northwestern frontier were warriors such as Naiwash of the Ottawas, who continued to assist the British following Tecumseh's death;[34] Shabbona, an Ottawa-Potawatomi who fought at Tecumseh's side at the Thames;[35] Black Hawk, the famous Sac war chief who participated in the attacks upon Forts Meigs and Stephenson;[36] Winimac, a pro-British Potawatomi who was killed following the unsuccessful siege of Fort Wayne;[37] Pakoisheecan of the Kickapoos, who led the attack upon Fort Harrison;[38] and Dog Head, who led the Winnebagoes at the Battle of Tippecanoe, and also assisted Colonel Robert McDouall in Wisconsin.[39]

Yet none of the above hold the magnetism of Tecumseh. For if either the Americans or the British could have designed an Indian leader, it would have been the Shawnee. For whites, he has always epitomized the "noble savage," and in the eyes of American, Canadian, or European historians, all the other Indians of his time paled by comparison. With his death, so died the Indian cause, and even the Prophet, who survived the war, so faded into obscurity that when he died in November 1836, few Americans knew or even cared about his passing.[40]

HAROLD D. LANGLEY

The Quest for Peace in the War of 1812

When the United States declared war on Great Britain on June 18, 1812, it was an act of desperation. Efforts to achieve respect for American rights had failed, as well as attempts at economic coercion. Unbeknownst to the Congress, a new ministry in Great Britain repealed the obnoxious Orders in Council on June 25, 1812, and with it the paper blockade of 1806 insofar as it concerned the Americans. One of the chief causes of the war was thus removed by the time the news of the declaration of war had reached Great Britain. For a time after that, British commanders tried to arrange for an armistice in the belief that there was no longer a cause for war. But the Madison administration did not support these overtures.[1]

On the same day that the British repealed their Orders in Council, Napoleon's army invaded Russia. Both the czar of Russia and the British government wondered if the American declaration of war meant that the United States was now an ally of France. When asked, John Quincy Adams, the American minister to Russia, assured the czar that the United States would not form any close connection with France. With the permission of Adams, the czar transmitted this information to the British Ambassador, Lord Cathcart, who had just arrived at St. Petersburg. Despite the fact that their nations were at war, Lord Cathcart left his card at Adams's house, and Adams returned the call. Both diplomats expressed the wish that the differences between their nations might be settled amicably.

In his conversation with Adams, the czar also asked if the United States would agree to accept Russian mediation in the War of 1812. The American said yes even though he had no authority to make such a promise.[2] Subsequently, President Madison agreed to such a mediation, and a delegation was named. It consisted of Albert Gallatin, secretary of the Treasury, and Senator James A. Bayard, a Delaware Federalist. These men proceeded to St. Petersburg, where they expected to work with Adams and the czar. They reached St. Petersburg in July 1813. Meanwhile, the British turned down the czar's offer, and in September 1813 the Russian ruler made a second offer of mediation. It was not until late October 1813 that the Americans in Russia learned that the British had again rejected the czar's offer. The British government had no desire to have the Russian ruler become involved in the Anglo-American family quarrel.

But in rejecting the czar's offer of mediation, British Foreign Secretary Lord Castlereagh was under pressure to institute direct talks with the Americans. On November 4, 1813, Castlereagh wrote to Secretary of State James Monroe that Great Britain was willing to negotiate "for a conciliatory adjustment of the differences subsisting between the two states, with an earnest desire to bring them to a favorable issue, upon principles of perfect reciprocity, not inconsistent with the established maxims of Public Law, and the maritime rights of the British Empire."[3] In other words, the British would negotiate but would not discuss the principles behind the Orders in Council or the practice of impressment. Madison and Monroe discussed this proposal and accepted its terms on January 5, 1814. Negotiations were to take place at Gothenburg, Sweden, but the locale was later changed to Ghent in the Netherlands. These arrangements called for a new diplomatic delegation, for Gallatin was expected back at the Treasury and Bayard at the Senate. The new commissioners were Henry Clay, Speaker of the House, and Jonathan Russell, lately U.S. Chargé des Affaires at London and now minister-designate to Sweden. They would be joined by John Quincy Adams. As things turned out, Gallatin and Bayard did not go home. Instead, they went to London where, in their unofficial capacity, they gained insights into the British outlook on the war and affairs in Europe and America. Later Gallatin and Bayard were added to the peace delegation. All of the Americans were assembled in Ghent on July 6, 1814, ready to begin the peace talks.

In the meantime great events had transpired in Europe. Napoleon's invasion of Russia had turned into a disaster. Upon leaving that country, he found himself faced with a powerful coalition that was determined to put an end to the menace of Napoleon. When the allied armies occupied Paris in mid-April 1814, Napoleon was sent off in exile to the island of

Elba. With Napoleon out of the way, it was clear that the British were going to increase the tempo, the range, and the stakes of the war in America. Bright prospects loomed before them, and savoring a taste for revenge, the British were in no hurry to begin peace discussions with the Americans. Eventually, a peace delegation was chosen and made its way to Ghent.

Historians have usually written off the British delegation as a group of third-raters, whose task was really to transmit messages and to leave the big decisions to others. Certainly, they were not as distinguished as their American colleagues, but they did have some qualifications that would be useful for spinning out negotiations until the British were ready to settle. Henry Goulbourn, a member of Parliament, had served as an under secretary of state for Home Affairs, for War, and for the Colonies. He was thus in a position to know something about how various issues and solutions might be perceived in Parliament, on the homefront, and in the colonies. John Quincy Adams thought he was the "ablest and toughest" of the three British commissioners. There was also William Adams, a graduate of Oxford, a doctor of civil law, and a specialist in admiralty law. He would be a valuable resource if the Americans chose to bring up old treaties, practices, or esoteric points of law. Such discussions might well have consumed a great deal of time and accomplished nothing except to buttress the British case. "What is wanted," said Castlereagh, "is a man of legal mind and of a very accurate understanding."[4] Adams met those criteria. Finally, there was James Lord Gambier, late Admiral of the White, now Admiral of the Red.[5] Although not well-known to Americans, Gambier had acquired the reputation of being a friend of the British seamen. He could at least listen and present his own anecdotes in any talk about impressment.

The first meeting of the two delegations took place on August 8. The Americans expected to discuss the definitions of blockade, neutral rights, the indemnities for the seizure of ships and cargoes, impressment, and the end of British trade with the Indians. Instead, they were told that some revisions in the Canadian-American boundary would be necessary. The past privilege of letting American fishermen dry their catches on Canadian coasts would not be renewed unless some suitable equivalent was granted by the United States. The pending treaty must give satisfactory boundaries to Britain's Indian allies. There were also indications that the British intended to establish a naval dominance on the Great Lakes.

In his response to the British propositions, John Quincy Adams pointed out that the Americans were prepared to discuss impressment and natural boundaries, but not the fisheries, peace with the Indians, or Indian boundaries. The latter points had not been matters of dispute between the nations.

In the weeks that followed, it became clear that the British wanted to separate the Indians from American sovereignty and to create a buffer state in the Old Northwest. This Indian domain would take in most of Ohio, Indiana, Illinois, Wisconsin, and Michigan, or about one third of the territory of the United States. Some hundred thousand white settlers in the area would have to be moved. The British wanted the northeast boundary altered so that there would be a direct route from Halifax to Quebec. In addition they wanted a boundary between Lake Superior and the Mississippi River revised so that there would be access to the river and the freedom of navigation of it. The sheer magnitude of the British territorial demands were such that all other questions, such as impressment, the fisheries, and indemnities for captures, became secondary issues.

The Americans were stunned by these proposals and by the British statement that they were the prerequisites for other discussions. There was no doubt about the American reply. They could not accept propositions that circumscribed the nation's sovereignty, sullied its honor, and took huge amounts of its territory. That would be a surrender. It would be better to have the war go on for a knowledge of the alternative would surely unify Americans as never before. Both the American and British delegations believed that negotiations would be broken off.

But the British government was not in favor of so drastic a step. Among other things, breaking off negotiations would involve a Parliamentary scrutiny of not only the proceedings but particularly the areas of contention. Instead, the British hoped to play for time, confident that the campaigns of 1814 in America would result in British victories and hence an even stronger negotiating position. As Prime Minister Lord Liverpool expressed it: "If our commander does his duty, I am persuaded we shall have acquired by our arms every point on the Canadian frontier which we ought to insist on keeping."[6] British optimism seemed to be borne out by the news of the capture of Washington and of the movement against Baltimore. It seemed likely that the United States government would soon be forced to sue for peace. Already that government was nearly bankrupt, and it faced the prospect that the New England states might secede from the Union. If that happened, New England would make a separate peace with Britain. A few more military setbacks would make the Americans more receptive to territorial demands and to unilateral disarmament on the Great Lakes.

Yet in the midst of this period of anticipation, the British dropped their demands for a unilateral disarmament on the Great Lakes and said that the proposal in regard to the Indians was no longer a requirement for continuing the negotiations. This alteration in the instructions to the British delegation was the result of Lord Liverpool's change of mind. If the peace talks broke down, Liverpool did not want it to be over the Great Lakes or the Indians. An unyielding stance on these issues might be hard to justify to the ministry's opponents in Parliament. For their part, the American delegation accepted the British demand that peace with the Indians be a part of the larger settlement. But they accepted this only as a provisional article, and one that could be accepted or rejected in Washington. Liverpool was nevertheless pleased with the American response. Thus far the Americans had been quite unreasonable. Some military reverses in the United States would make them more realistic and receptive to the British terms.

In Ghent the Americans did not respond quite the way that Liverpool had expected. Notwithstanding the bad news of the capture of Washington and fears that additional reverses might lie ahead, the Americans held firmly to their convictions. Later reports brought the good news that Baltimore did not fall, and that a squadron under Commodore Thomas MacDonough had stopped a British invasion of New York State by way of Lake Champlain. Despite the change in their military expectations, the British instructed their delegation to insist that the peace be based on the doctrine of *uti possidetus,* or each side retaining the territory it held at the time the treaty was signed. But the American delegation absolutely refused to consider any treaty on such a basis.

The American rejection of the doctrine of *uti possidetus* deeply disturbed Lord Liverpool. It seemed to him that these men simply refused to accept reality. Given their stance, it now seemed likely that the war in America would have to continue for a while longer. In that case, Britain's Continental allies would probably be sympathetic to the United States. The czar was already regarded as pro-American. Liverpool, therefore, advised Castlereagh to cease his opposition to the czar's occupation of Poland, and to make no new enemies at Vienna.

If the situations in Vienna and Ghent were not disturbing enough, there were also worries about France. King Louis XVIII, who had replaced Napoleon as the head of state, was not acceptable to many Frenchmen. There was unrest in France and threats against the king. How long would it take to stabilize France? If there was a fresh outbreak of fighting on the Continent, the British must see it through to the end.

Continuing the war in America would mean a new loan and a continuance of a property tax that was already unpopular. What might be required if war had to be waged both in America and on the Continent? It was not a pleasant prospect to contemplate. Could anything be done to change the situation?

On October 31, the British requested the Americans at Ghent to prepare their own draft treaty. The Americans had anticipated such a request and were struggling to reach an agreement. Instructions from Washington had freed them from the need to press the issues of impressment, indemnities for captures, or neutral rights. But since the British had said that the liberty to fish in Canadian waters would not be restored without some American equivalent, this matter had to be addressed. There was also the British demand for the free navigation of the Mississippi. The discussions on the issues exposed the sectional points of view of the members of the group and put great strains on their sense of unity. In such a tense environment, the personal habits, idiosyncrasies, and political values of the delegates became matters of concern and comment. Despite such distractions, the Americans prepared a draft treaty and sent it with a note offering to make peace on the basis of the principle of *status quo ante bellum,* or the situation as it was before the war. This meant that nothing was said about the British navigation of the Mississippi, and it was assumed that the liberty to fish (given in the Treaty of Paris of 1783 ending the American Revolution) could not be revoked as a result of the declaration of war in 1812.

The first part of the draft treaty called for an end of hostilities and the mutual restoration of prisoners, territory, private and public property, and records. Then came an article that dealt with the time frame in which warfare would cease once the treaty was ratified. The next three articles dealt with the appointment of postwar commissions to determine the boundaries of Maine and then on to the St. Lawrence River, through the Great Lakes, and from Lake Superior to the Lake of the Woods. Conclusions based on the work of the commissions would put at rest disputes that had arisen since the treaty of 1783. The appointment of commissioners, their powers, duties and costs, were also addressed in these articles. A special article was devoted to the task of establishing the international boundary from the Lake of the Woods to the 49th parallel and then westward to the Rocky Mountains. In effect, this article would prevent any British access to the Mississippi River. Article nine incorporated the agreement already reached on peace with the Indians. This was followed by an article stating that both powers should restrain the

Indians living within their boundaries from committing hostilities against the other nation, and that in any future war neither side would use them. The proposition was thus a reflection of the oratory of the War Hawks about one of the causes of the war. Likewise, article eleven stipulated the temporary prohibition of the practice of impressment, and article twelve restricted the use of blockades. Next came the demand for indemnities for American citizens who suffered losses prior to the war for illegal captures, seizures, or condemnations. Article fourteen gave immunity to those persons on either side who had aided the enemy. The last article dealt with the ratification of the treaty. Once a clean copy of the draft was completed, it and the all-important note offering to settle on the basis of *status quo ante bellum* were delivered to the British commissioners as they were preparing to retire for the night.

Meanwhile in London, Lord Liverpool, angered by the earlier American rejection of the doctrine of *uti posseditus* and concerned about the signs of a mounting domestic reaction to high taxes, as well as the unrest in France, searched for a solution to his problems. At a cabinet meeting on November 3, it seemed wise to remove Wellington from his post as minister to France and give him the command of military operations in America. Wellington would surely bring matters there to a satisfactory conclusion. Liverpool wrote to Wellington about the proposition. Before the duke could reply, there was more disturbing news from Vienna. Castlereagh ignored the prime minister's instructions that he should be friendly to the czar, and instead persisted in his stand that the Russian troops must get out of Poland. Otherwise, European stability would again be threatened. With these problems as a background, Wellington gave to Liverpool the benefit of his thoughts.

To Wellington it seemed clear that he could not go to America at this time, for if trouble arose on the Continent, "there is nobody but myself in whom either yourselves or your country or your Allies, would feel any confidence."[7] As for the situation in America, it was a question of whether Britain could attain a naval superiority on the Great Lakes. If it could not, then there would be little point in Wellington going there. Britain's military operations did not entitle it to make any territorial demands. Indeed such demands would give the Americans an excuse to break off the peace negotiations. Ultimately a peace might have to be signed without a British military victory. If so, then a peace might as well be signed now on the basis of *status quo ante bellum.*

Wellington's reply was received by Liverpool about the same time as the American draft treaty and the comments thereon by the British commissioners. A few days later, newspapers and letters arrived from

America containing information that the Madison administration had published a record of the British peace proposals down through the end of August. These sources indicated that the terms had so infuriated the Americans that there were indications of a new unity and resolution to resist the British. Even a Federalist congressman, who was normally sympathetic to the British, was dismayed by the terms. Lord Liverpool was angry that Madison had published the earlier proposals not only for what it did for the American cause, but because it gave Britain's Whigs valuable information with which to attack their political rivals. On top of this came charges from the Admiralty against the British army for the way in which naval forces were misused on Lake Erie and Lake Champlain. There were increasingly disturbing reports from Paris and Vienna about the political situations in those capitals. Liverpool called his cabinet together on November 18 to decide what should be done.

As a result of these discussions, Castlereagh was advised that it was now considered desirable to bring the war in America to a conclusion. The British commissioners at Ghent were informed that their government accepted the proposition of a peace based on the *status quo ante bellum,* and would not discuss the question of the fisheries. The international, financial, and domestic reasons for the change in tactics were noted. Faced with the need to conclude the war as soon as possible, the British commissioners worked over the American draft treaty amending, rewording, and eliminating phrases and articles. Their handiwork was then delivered to the American delegation.

An examination of the amended draft showed that the articles on blockade, impressment, indemnities, the supervision of the Indians, and amnesty had been rejected. This came as no great surprise. More serious were the British efforts to get free navigation of the Mississippi, to determine the direction of the line drawn from the Lake of the Woods, to deny the liberty to fish, and to claim ownership of the Passamaquoddy Islands off the coast of Maine. Once again the American delegates reflected their sectional points of view in discussions over the navigation of the Mississippi and a provision for fishing in Canadian waters, as well as the ownership of the disputed islands. Gradually they worked their way to a consensus. Adams and Gallatin drafted an article giving the British access to the upper Mississippi subject to the payment of customs duties. The Americans also decided to have the article on indemnity cover only the first six months of the war, and to omit any mention of the sale of captured Negro slaves.

It was now time for the two delegations to sit down and to reach a final decision on the treaty. Such meetings took place on December 1,

10, and 12. Before they were completed, the men from both delegations had grown weary of the long discussions over various matters. Their comments were sent to London and to Washington where there were other conversations. On December 13 and 14, the American delegation worked by themselves on the content of what they hoped would be their final note to the British. They were still worried that the negotiations might break down.

In the end the questions that could not be resolved were left to special postwar commissions. These included the fisheries, the northeastern boundary of the United States, the ownership of the islands in Passamaquoddy Bay, and the river and lake boundary on the north. The British accepted these arrangements. They gave up on the navigation of the Mississippi. A meeting of both delegations followed on December 23. This was devoted to slight changes in the wording of some points. The Americans were angry about a proposal that the debts incurred by American prisoners of war in Great Britain and paid in paper must be repaid in specie. Gallatin said that the British would make a profit of 10 to 12 percent on the deal, and Adams estimated that it was more like 15 percent. But they agreed to it reluctantly. Adams and his colleagues were successful in eliminating a British article that would keep the courts of both countries open for the claims of each nation. They failed in their efforts to strike out an article denouncing the slave trade and the promise that both nations would try to eliminate the practice. By three o'clock P.M. agreement had been reached on the wording of all the articles. Each commission now had to make three clean copies for the signing ceremony.

Negotiations that had gone on for nearly five months ended with the signing of the Treaty of Ghent on Christmas Eve 1814. In handing over the British copies of the treaty to John Quincy Adams, Admiral Gambier expressed the wish that the settlement would be permanent. Adams, in delivering his copies, said that he and his colleagues hoped that this would be the last peace treaty between the United States and Great Britain. So it proved to be. The treaty was promptly ratified by both countries.[8] The War of 1812 was over.

When the text of the treaty was printed in the newspapers, the citizenry of both countries had the opportunity to examine what had been done at Ghent. Americans saw that there was nothing about impressment, neutral rights, or indemnities—issues about which they went to war. For some it seemed that the prewar rights of the Indians were guaranteed; but in reality, most of the terms were concerned with the end of hostilities with them. Time would show that other guarantees were not very lasting. If any Americans were disappointed that they gained no territory in Canada, they could take consolation from the fact that they had lost none of their own lands. In time they would come to know that the absence of any statement about the navigation of the Mississippi River represented an important victory. For the British, the fact that the treaty did little more than restore the status quo was not an occasion for celebration. But both sides were relieved that the war was over.

The good work begun at Ghent was carried on by others. The Passamaquoddy Commission of 1817 divided the islands between the United States and Great Britain. Fishing grounds in the Canadian waters that the Americans could use were set forth in the Convention of 1818. But throughout the passage of time, the fisheries question would periodically emerge in Anglo-American relations, finally to be resolved in 1910. Boundary commissions and later treaties would eventually resolve the matter of the border between the United States and Canada. As minister to Great Britain after the war, John Quincy Adams raised with Castlereagh the question of naval disarmament on the Great Lakes. This led to the Rush-Bagot Agreement of 1817 limiting the number, size, and armament of the naval forces on the Lakes. Although only a small beginning, and not fully implemented until 1871, that treaty marked the start of the concept of the undefended border. How that dream became a reality is a matter of special interest to us today both as we remember Perry's victory at Lake Erie and as we celebrate 175 years of peace between the United States and Canada.[9]

IAN C. B. PEMBERTON

Historiography of the War of 1812: The Canadian View of the Battle of Lake Erie and Its Aftermath

For Canadian historians of the War of 1812, the Battle of Lake Erie and its immediate aftermath raise a major problem: how does one deal with the question of defeat and invasion? For the most part, the approach has been to isolate certain factors—Captain Robert Barclay's undermanned squadron, for instance, or the sins of omission and commission of Major-General Henry Procter—in explaining the disastrous events of September–October 1813. Canadian historians also pay considerable attention to the strategic results of Lake Erie and Moraviantown and have derived some satisfaction that Harrison and Perry were not able to capitalize more on their hard-won endeavors.

The historians chosen for this exercise reflect opinions over a broad spectrum of time. First in this procession was Major John Richardson who was a participant in the war and was taken prisoner at Moraviantown. His book, *Richardson's War of 1812,* republished in 1902, represented a contemporary Canadian view, albeit one written a number of years after the war. James Hannay, *A History of the War of 1812,* published in 1905, represented a turn-of-the-century view and was clearly the most anti-American of the works consulted. Fred Landon, *Western Ontario and the American Frontier,* first published in 1941, and Gerald Craig, *Upper Canada, the Formative Years, 1784–1841,* published in 1963, were included as examples of highly respected surveys which touched briefly on the events concerned here. J. Mackay Hitsman, *The Incredible War of 1812,* published in 1965, and George F. G. Stanley, *The War of 1812: Land Operations,* published in 1983, were strictly military histories. Pierre Berton, *Flames Across the Border, 1813–1814,* published in 1981, provided a lively popular account of the period and was the one volume which would likely be familiar to the general Canadian reader.

Periodical literature was also considered in this particular canvass. Ernest A. Cruikshank's article, "The Contest for the Command of Lake Erie in 1812–1813," was first published by the Royal Canadian Institute in 1899. C. P. Stacey, "Another Look at the Battle of Lake Erie," first appeared in the *Canadian Historical Review* of March 1958. Katherine B. Coutts's article, "Thamesville and the Battle of the Thames," appeared in 1908 in the *Papers and Records* of the Ontario Historical Society. Victor Lauriston, "The Case for General Procter," was published in 1951 by the Kent County Historical Society. Sandy Antal's article, "Myths and Facts Concerning General Procter," appeared in the September 1987 edition of *Ontario History*. Cruikshank and Stacey represent professional historians, the former being a pioneer in the writing of Ontario history, while the latter is one of Canada's foremost military historians. Coutts and Lauriston reflect a more popular format with Coutts's work in particular emphasizing an interest in local history. Captain Sandy Antal, an officer in the Canadian Armed Forces, is another professional historian with a decidedly revisionist view of Procter. With the exception of Antal's article, all of these items have been reprinted in Morris Zaslow's useful compilation, *The Defended Border: Upper Canada and the War of 1812*.

In examining how these various historians have viewed the Battle of Lake Erie and the subsequent Thames campaign, this study has concentrated on six major points. First of all, how has Captain Barclay and his problem of supply and manpower been viewed? Similarly, what has been the Canadian view of his opponent, Commodore Oliver Hazard Perry? Yet another question deals with how the local Canadian population responded to the turn of events which followed Barclay's defeat. Two more major areas of interest center on the actions and personalities of Tecumseh and Procter in this desperate time. Finally, an effort has been made to assess the strategic results of the American victories on Lake Erie and the Thames.

The first question—the situation of Captain Barclay during the summer of 1813—has drawn a considerable degree of unanimity from the scholars in question. There was a consensus that the young one-armed veteran of the Napoleonic Wars was in a very difficult situation. Perry was building his squadron at Presque Isle on the Pennsylvania shore of Lake Erie, and clearly a preventative raid was in order. Cruikshank summed up Barclay's problem nicely:

> Barclay again reconnoitered the harbour and ascertained that the two new brigs were still in the inner harbour, apparently in a forward state but not yet rigged. Besides these he noted two smaller brigs and

seven schooners, all of which appeared to be armed, manned, and ready for sea. Next day, he wrote from Long Point to the Governor-General complaining warmly of the want of seamen and stores. "The ships," he said, "are manned with crews, part of which cannot even speak English, and none of them seamen and very few in numbers."[1]

Broadly speaking, Hitsman, Craig, Berton, Stanley, and Stacey agree with this description, although the latter adds a couple of interesting and significant factors. Stacey underscores the tactical importance of the American raid on York (Toronto) in April 1813 that saw the destruction or seizure by the enemy of vital naval stores that would have been invaluable to Barclay. Secondly, Stacey stressed the facilities at Pittsburgh for boring cannon and making anchors and rope that he suggested gave the American commander an enormous logistical advantage. Barclay simply did not have such facilities at his command.[2]

Captain Barclay thus emerged as a concerned and hard-working individual who was hampered by his military and naval seniors on Lake Ontario. While James Hannay acknowledged these problems, he also suggested that Barclay may not have been quite as concerned with duty as he should have:

> At Amherstburg there was a pretty widow of an officer of some rank who was very anxious to get to York. Captain Barclay offered her a passage down the lake in his ship, conveyed her to Port Dover, and then escorted her to the residence of Dr. Rolph. Barclay was invited to a dinner there the following day and waited over to attend it. When he got back to Erie, after an absence of more than three days from his post, the American brigs were over the bar and the control of the Lake had passed from his hands.[3]

Beside the portrayal of British naval commander Barclay, the portrait which Canadian historians have drawn of Commodore Perry has also been, by and large, a positive one. Hitsman acknowledged that Perry was almost as short of seamen as was Barclay and for much the same reason—Commodore Chauncey on Lake Ontario was looking after his own needs first. Cruikshank noted that Perry was fully armed and equipped by July 10, "but he wisely refused to take the lake until provided with a sufficient complement of able seamen." Berton added a note of levity by observing that the American naval commander was deathly afraid of cows, that he would "trudge through mud to avoid one if he hears so much as a moo." Only James Hannay has injected a harsh note by suggesting that Perry's advantage was so enormous that the dramatics involved in raising his famous "DONT GIVE UP THE SHIP" flag were in rather poor taste:

> Yet, with the assurance of victory which his two-fold superiority gave him, Perry thought it necessary to increase the importance of his anticipated triumph by resorting to demonstrations of a theatrical character. He had a large flag prepared for his ship with the alleged dying words of Captain Lawrence, "Don't give up the ship," printed upon it, and in imitation of Nelson he called together the officers of his squadron to give them instructions with regard to the expected action. As the officers were leaving, he said: "Gentlemen, remember your instructions. Nelson has expressed my idea in the words, 'If you lay your enemy close alongside, you cannot be out of place,' good-night." Nelson expressing Perry's idea is something calculated to arouse the mirth of nations.[4]

Charles Stacey struck a note of balance when he gave Perry full marks for his conduct during the battle. The construction of the fleet, Stacey noted, owed considerable credit to Commodore Chauncey and Secretary of the Navy Jones, as well as Perry himself. However, the victory itself was uniquely Perry's: "At the crisis of the fight, when an engagement which ought never to have been in doubt was close to being lost through no fault of his, it was the young commander's energy and resolution that saved the day; but for him the outcome would have been different." Berton has related the humane side of Perry in the aftermath of victory—assisting the badly injured Barclay to attend a special service for the officers of both sides and then sitting with him on the *Detroit* until the British commander had fallen asleep. "Now that the heat of battle has passed, he looks on his foes without rancor, makes sure his officers treat them well, urges Washington to grant Barclay an immediate and unconditional parole so that he may recover."[5]

How did the Canadian population living in the farthest extremes of southwestern Ontario react to this stunning change in the fortunes of the war? Canadian historians have been remarkably coy on the subject. Stanley makes mention of Harrison detailing one of his officers to open talks with disaffected Indians at Detroit. He also refers to a deserter from the Canadian militia who lived on the Thames below Moraviantown, Matthew Dolson, as having agreed to serve the Americans as a guide. Hitsman claimed that most residents in the path of the invasion simply kept a low profile and hoped that their homes would not be looted. Berton rather primly referred to the withdrawal of "those white settlers who do not wish to remain under foreign rule."[6] Virtually nothing else has been recorded by any of the historians chosen for this selection. The absence of material on this vital point is interesting and does raise the question whether perhaps there is not herein a subject worthy of additional investigation.

On the dreary retreat from Amherstburg to Moraviantown and in the subsequent battle at that site, one figure stands out in heroic proportions: Tecumseh. Virtually all the sources praised his leadership and his humanity. Richardson would note: "The most serious loss we sustained on this occasion [Moraviantown] was that of the noble and unfortunate Tecumseh." Katherine Coutts declared: "Yet from the day Tecumseh took his stand beside Brock at Detroit till that on which [Colonel Richard] Johnson's bullet stilled forever his noble heart, he never wavered in his determination and loyalty." Stanley credited the great Shawnee with keeping the Indians in the fight at Moraviantown after the British had either surrendered or fled: "Wounded several times, Tecumseh refused to give up. When [William] Caldwell saw him using his rifle as a crutch and questioned him, Tecumseh showed Caldwell a gaping chest wound. But he still fought on." Pierre Berton has dramatically captured Tecumseh's leadership of his people during the last moments of his life:

> One man, the Kentuckians know, is in charge: they can hear Tecumseh's terrible battle cry piercing the ragged wall of sound. For five years they have heard its echo, ever since the Shawnee first made his presence felt in the Northwest. Yet that presence has always been spectral: no Kentuckian on the field this day—no white American, in fact, save Harrison—has ever seen the Shawnee chief or heard his voice until this moment. He is a figure of legend, his origins clouded in myth, his persona a reflection of other men's perception.[7]

One of the persistent legends of Tecumseh revolves around the story that his body was never found on the field of battle at Moraviantown. Berton has made much of this issue in his account: "No headstone, marker, or monument will identify his resting place. His followers have spirited him away to a spot where no stranger, be he British or American, will ever find him—his earthly clay, like his own forlorn hope, buried forever in a secret grave." Unfortunately, John Richardson, who was himself taken prisoner and who presumably had no reason to distort the record, told a different story:

> It has been asserted that the mutilated remains which were supposed to have been his, were in reality those of another chief. Would for the honor of humanity it had been so: but this is incorrect. Several of the officers of the 41st, on being apprized of his fall, went, accompanied by some of General Harrison's staff, to visit the spot where Tecumseh lay, and there they identified (for they knew him well) in the mangled corpse before them all that remained of the late powerful and intelligent chief.[8]

One might perhaps suggest that the officers were simply co-conspirators in a spontaneous effort to protect Tecumseh's identity. In any event, Tecumseh lives on as one of the few heroes to Canadians from this dark period of the War of 1812. Pierre Berton, never at a loss for a dramatic flourish, sums up this view well: "in death as in life, there is only one Tecumseh . . . [and] his memory will be for ever green."[9]

If Tecumseh emerges triumphant from this page of Canadian history, Major-General Henry Procter most assuredly does not. Procter was the commander who fled from Amherstburg and Detroit without firing a shot after Barclay's defeat and then conducted a disorderly retreat up the Thames to defeat at Moraviantown, a battle from which he departed with his family during the early stages of the fighting. He subsequently blamed his troops for the defeat. John Richardson made no effort to hide his disgust: "Yet this man . . . turns upon his gallant supporters in the moment of their misfortune, and, in his base attempt to redeem his own blighted military reputation, scruples not to charge them with misconduct in the field."[10]

As Richardson set the basic standard, others fell into line behind him. Stanley spoke of Procter's command "going to pieces" during the retreat up the Thames. Even such an elementary step as the burning of bridges to hold up the enemy was apparently forgotten. Lieutenant-Colonel Augustus Warburton, Procter's second-in-command, was left to manage the operation while Procter, far to the front, with his family and the heavy baggage, offered little direction. Hitsman simply described Procter as "inept as a field commander," while Cruikshank accused him of "indecision and unpardonable negligence." Katherine Coutts flayed him roundly in her article on Thamesville, suggesting that he was sacrificing his troops "as the wicked man in the children's story flung the child from his arms to the wolves."[11] It is little wonder that to this day Procter's name has not been a popular one in naming schools and shopping malls or even streets in southwestern Ontario.

Despite the bad esteem in which he is generally held, Henry Procter has had his defenders. James Hannay has suggested that Procter drew up his army for battle with considerable skill, and that he conducted a successful retreat from Moraviantown which saw 246 men and officers escape to Ancaster on Lake Ontario. According to Hannay, Procter was a victim of the unreliability of his Indian allies. "It is easy to see at this day," Hannay claims, "that Procter was unjustly condemned."[12]

Another spirited defense of Procter has come from the pen of Victor Lauriston who felt that this man was the victim of a variety of unfortunate circumstances. He blamed a number of factors for Procter's unhappy fate—the ignorance of his superiors, the unreliability of the Indians, and the venom of Major Richardson. In effect, Lauriston argued that Procter did the best he could under dreadful circumstances, and that he has been made one of history's scapegoats. His thesis is an interesting one, but one cannot help but wonder if Procter really faced his task at Moraviantown "in the intrepid spirit of Brock" as his apologist suggests.[13]

A modern scholar who has come to Procter's defense is Captain Sandy Antal. His interesting and well-researched article covered some familiar ground—the uncooperative attitude of Procter's superiors and the unreliability of the Indians—but also suggested that Richardson was strongly and unjustifiably biased against his commander and that he has thus prejudiced much of subsequent Canadian opinion. Antal made extensive use of Procter's court-martial proceedings which, he argued, put his embattled subject in a much more favorable light. The author pointed out that such apparently sloppy acts as leaving bridges intact was to facilitate the escape of the families of the Indians; had the bridges been burned, the Indians unquestionably would have turned on the British. On balance, Antal felt that a careful and impartial examination of the facts would show that Procter was anything but a bungler and that he had been very largely instrumental in the defense of southwestern Ontario during the first year of the war.[14]

Perhaps the most balanced appraisal of Procter was that provided by Pierre Berton:

> To the Americans he remains a monster, to the Canadians a coward. He is neither—merely a victim of circumstances, a brave officer but weak, capable enough except in moments of stress, a man of modest pretensions, unable to make the quantum leap that distinguishes the outstanding leader from the run-of-the-mill: the quality of being able in moments of adversity to exceed one's own capabilities. The prisoner of events beyond his control, Procter dallied and equivocated until he was crushed. His career is ended.[15]

One cannot help but feel that there might be grounds for a revisionist biography of Procter, although clearly it would be a significant challenge against the crust of the traditional view.

How have Canadian historians interpreted the results of these two major American triumphs? Landon noted the precarious position of the British post on Mackinac Island which had been taken from the Americans early in the war. He also observed, as did Hitsman, that General Prevost was prepared to abandon Upper Canada as far east as Kingston in the wake of these twin disasters. Berton stressed the point that the Indian lands of the Northwest were now ripe for the taking.[16] However, the observation which most of the authors made was that the Americans did very little to exploit their opportunity, even failing to recapture Mackinac in the summer of 1814.

George Stanley was particularly impressed with this development: "Complete as Harrison's victory was, it did not lead to strategic success." Stanley's explanation centered on two factors: Harrison had outmarched his line of communication, and heavy autumn rains had turned already bad Canadian roads into a quagmire. Hannay described the American withdrawal to the Detroit River with a certain undertone of satisfaction at the terrible conditions which the victors were forced to endure—perhaps God was an Englishman after all: "They arrived at Sandwich on the tenth, in the midst of a furious storm of wind and snow, during which several of the vessels from the Thames were injured and much of the captured property lost. Thus, ended the campaign." In a somewhat similar vein, Cruikshank noted that a number of the ships of Perry's squadron were subsequently taken at Buffalo, Fort Erie, and Mackinac: "Practically the only service of much consequence performed by the American squadron was the conveyance of a body of troops to Long Point (May 14, 1814) and covering the landing of a division of their army at Fort Erie (July 3, 1814)." Craig suggested that the American withdrawal was "unaccountable," but was on stronger ground with his concluding statement: "His [Harrison's] victory ended the Indian menace in the Michigan-Indiana region once and for all, and did something to strengthen the hands of American diplomats at the subsequent peace conference, but it proved not to be a mortal blow at the security of the province."[17] In the final analysis, the latter point surely represented the bottom line for Canadians.

Perhaps because the defeats on Lake Erie and on the Thames did not prove to be fatal to the British hold on Canada, Canada's historians of the War of 1812 have on the whole maintained a reasonably balanced perspective of this dire period in their history. By emphasizing Barclay's difficulties, Perry's advantages, and Procter's inadequacies, they have satisfied themselves as to why events unfolded the way they did in the fall of 1813. They have found consolation by laying claim to the martyred Tecumseh and by suggesting, with an occasional malicious chuckle, that the Americans might have won a couple of battles but they did not win the war. Finally, they have done relatively little to reveal how Canadians themselves reacted to these events at the time. They have performed some valuable spade work for us, and with that sense of courtesy for which Canadians are renowned, have left enough unanswered questions to occupy at least one more generation.

CHRISTOPHER McKEE

An Aerial View of Put-in-Bay: United States Historians Scrutinize a Campaign

What does a historian do when the responsibility is to summarize, in far less time than it took to fight the battle, what United States commentators have written during the past 175 years about Oliver Hazard Perry's victory on Lake Erie?

Sheer mass is an excellent reason for concern. More than 6,000 books and articles are cited in John C. Fredriksen's *Free Trade and Sailors' Rights: A Bibliography of the War of 1812* (1985). Nearly two hundred of these pertain directly to the Battle of Lake Erie. Beyond these there exists an uncounted mass of more general works in which a reader might find significant discussion of the battle, of the events leading up to it, or of its consequences. But just as one has, in flying over Lake Erie at 25,000 feet, a better appreciation of the geography of the battle, so also a high-altitude scholarly overflight can enable the historian to discover the main threads of United States writings about the Battle of Lake Erie, even though one has trouble disentangling the Battle of Lake Erie threads from the more general story of the war, by land and by sea, along the northern frontier. Not only is the mass of existing publications dismaying, but the subject—the historiography of the Battle of Lake Erie—offers a perverse temptation to enlarge one's mandate to include what historians have *not,* but perhaps should have, written about the battle and the larger campaign of which it was a part. After 175 years of studying the Battle of Lake Erie is there anything new left to say? Yes, definitely.

The first thread is that of the general histories of the War of 1812, in which larger context the Battle of Lake Erie must be placed and appraised.[1] For Alfred Thayer Mahan (*Sea Power in Its Relations to the War of 1812* [1905]), the destruction of the British naval force on September

10, 1813, decided the campaign in the northwest by transferring control of the inland waters to the United States forces. According to Mahan the military results thus achieved were final. "Nothing occurred to modify them during the rest of the war." Detroit and the Michigan Territory were restored to the United States. "Indian terror" in the northwest territories was permanently laid to rest.[2] Mahan's is a fair summary of the traditional position assumed by United States historians respecting the outcome of the battles of Lake Erie and the Thames. He conveniently ignores the reality that, de facto, the British/Canadian forces did retain mastery of the upper lakes and the territory west of Lake Michigan for the balance of the war—and that even United States control of Lake Erie had become tenuous by the end of 1814.

A more recent view is enunciated by J. C. A. Stagg in *Mr. Madison's War: Politics, Diplomacy, and Warfare in the Early American Republic, 1783–1830* (1983). Stagg sees the 1813 battles as one more tilt of the seesaw, this time in favor of the United States. It was a three-year series of ups and downs that ultimately made the war a zero sum game—an outcome that perhaps made the best possible contribution to the future mutual tolerance, if not happiness, of the two nations whose shared border runs across the water of Lake Erie.

Assessing who won what in war is a tricky business. From the perspective of 175 years it seems to this historian that the Battle of Lake Erie's uncontestable legacy to the young United States was reinforcement of a growing national self-confidence and sense of identity. More narrowly, Lake Erie and other maritime victories in the War of 1812 gave a tremendous élan to the growth and professional stability of the young United States Navy. The lakes campaigns in particular demonstrated that, when the two navies started out with approximately equal numbers of poker chips, the new American force was well able to hold its own against the older and more powerful British parent. The Erie battle's mythic importance in the United States Navy's sense of itself and its history may perhaps be greater than any tangible outcome of the campaign of 1813.

These authors, for whom Mahan and Stagg stand representative, were each and all writing general histories of the war. The Battle of Lake Erie was only a small part of a larger story. Here is one of the strangest gaps in United States historical writing: the lack of a book which focuses primarily on the War of 1812 on the lakes frontier. These northern campaigns were sufficiently isolated from the rest of the war so that telling their story separately does little violence to historical reality. Extending from Lake Champlain to Lake Superior, with battles on land and on water, brimming with dramatic events, alive with memorable personalities, exhibiting spectacular and abysmal examples of army-navy cooperation and antagonism—this warfare would present a marvelous subject to a latter-day Arthur Marder, a historian able to master all of these themes, see how they relate to one another, and weave them into one engrossing narrative. Such a book will not be written as though the Battle of Lake Erie was the end of the war on the upper lakes. It will explore why discipline fell apart at the United States base at Presque Isle in the winter of 1813–14, chart how the United States failed to exploit its initial strategic advantage on the upper lakes in the campaign of 1814, trace the actual loss of control on Lake Huron, and delineate that dangerously thin spider's web by which United States mastery of Lake Erie hung suspended at the end of 1814.

A second major thread of United States historical writing is the strand labeled biographical studies. Indeed, as far as the biographers are concerned, there was only one man at the Battle of Lake Erie: Oliver Hazard Perry. For me, the best work is still Alexander Slidell Mackenzie's 1840 *Life of Commodore Oliver Hazard Perry.* Easy enough to dismiss these dull-looking little green volumes as dated nineteenth-century writing, to be honored but not to be read. A perhaps wiser view sees Mackenzie's *Perry* as a work of the highest scholarly and literary standards, still eminently approachable. More problematic, for the scholar at least, is the most recent entry in the field, Richard Dillon's *We Have Met the Enemy: Oliver Hazard Perry, Wilderness Commodore* (1978), a book which sank from sight as it ran off the end of the launching ways. Indeed, *We Have Met the Enemy* went down so fast that it was not even observed and reported in the historical reviewing literature of the day. For scholars the problem with Dillon's book is that, although the author was a careful, accurate historian, who seemingly worked from previously untapped manuscript sources, the book can be searched from cover to cover without finding a hint—no footnotes, no bibliography, no essay—of what those sources may have been and where they are. Because of its strange fate—a kind of scholarly cruiser *Indianapolis,* if you will—Dillon's book is likely to have little impact on the collective appreciation of the Battle of Lake Erie in years to come.

In their enthusiasm for their hero, all Perry biographers avoid an essential point: the devastating effect of Perry's self-centeredness on the later conduct of the war. The battle won, Perry could scarcely wait to get himself removed from the lakes frontier to what he perceived to be more desirable duty on the eastern seaboard. His sole concerns seemed to be his own convenience and a frantic search for greater opportunities to distinguish himself on the ocean, a search in which success eluded him for the balance of his life. The loss of Perry's dynamic and effective leadership led directly to the unraveling in 1814 of the United States gains of 1813.

The only historian who has acknowledged that any human beings worthy of recollection, other than Perry, fought at the battle off Put-in-Bay was Usher Parsons, whose *Brief Sketches of the Officers Who Were in the Battle of Lake Erie,* published in 1862, was the first and last attempt—two or three short pieces on Daniel Dobbins and Stephen Champlin aside—to tell the stories of any of Perry's officer subordinates. A number of these neglected lieutenants deserve to be resurrected, but the failure of biographers to study one man is, to me, inexplicable. I am referring to Jesse Duncan Elliott.

Mention of Elliott's name brings us to the third thread in United States historical writing about the battle: controversial literature praising, defending, or excoriating Elliott's role in the events of September 1813, of which outpouring James Fenimore Cooper's *The Battle of Lake Erie* (1843) is the most famous piece. Generally speaking, this sort of after-the-fact clobbering in print is vitally interesting only to the participants in an event and their immediate partisans. (Witness the more recent Pearl Harbor controversy, for example.) Once the last living participant leaves the stage, the genre dies a natural death. In retrospect it may seem outrageously partisan, juvenile, or boring beyond belief. The reason I find it dreary to the point of unreadability is because all of the tens of thousands of words written fail to get at the heart of the matter. Jesse Duncan Elliott was a complex, strange, and possibly sick man. What Elliott did or failed to do on September 10, 1813, and why he behaved in such a manner are beyond the reach of the customary historical sources studied with conventional historical tools. One fervently hopes that some day a highly skilled practitioner of the psychohistorian's craft will take on the task of mastering the extensive sources respecting Elliott and offer (at last) a convincing and consistent explanation of this fascinating, albeit inscrutable, figure.[3]

If the officers who fought at the Battle of Lake Erie have been sadly neglected, the enlisted participants are wholly ignored. Muster rolls, seamen's protective certificates, prisoner-of-war registers, pension applications, court-martial transcripts, census records, memoirs, and reminiscences should make it possible for historians to discover where the enlisted men came from, what became of them after the battle, and how they recalled and evaluated their experience in the lakes campaigns as they sought to establish perspective and discover pattern in their lives.

When their story is written, health and sickness will be a significant theme, for wellness or its absence was a major factor in the conduct of the War of 1812 on the lakes. The Battle of Lake Erie was fought by sick men; some were too ill to fight. Specialized studies, then, are a fourth thread in United States writing about the battle. Max Rosenberg's *The Building of Perry's Fleet on Lake Erie, 1812–1813* (1950) is a good example of this type of history. Urgently required is a modern study, written by a qualified medical historian, of the role of morbidity and mortality in the conduct of war on the lakes frontier. Difficult as it may be, 175 years later, to appreciate that other, lost reality, the fact is that the lakes frontier was a problematic theater of operations during the War of 1812 because of major health problems endemic to the region. This was well known to contemporary medical participants, who began writing about their wartime challenges and experiences before the last gun had cooled and the last typhus victim had been hastily interred. Since that day awareness of this vital aspect of the war has waned. Whether a medical history of the war on the lakes frontier is integrated into the general history of the war in that theater or whether it comes in the form of a separate book, such a work, written to the highest standards of medical historical scholarship, is a priority need.

Fundamental to the pursuit of the several threads identified in writings about the Battle of Lake Erie is the availability of reliable sources. In this fifth category, documentary editing, scholars on the United States side of the border have lagged behind their Canadian counterparts. The latter could point with pride to William Wood's splendid four volumes of *Select British Documents of the Canadian War of 1812* (1920–28). The sole United States contribution was Charles O. Paullin's 1918 publication: *The Battle of Lake Erie: A Collection of Documents, Chiefly by Commodore Perry.* Paullin met the best standards of scholarship, but his beautifully printed volume was limited in its scope and published in so tiny an edition as to be virtually unobtainable except to the most fanatically persistent of bibliophiles. United States scholars are now making up for past deficiencies. In 1985 William S. Dudley and his colleagues at the Naval Historical Center in Washington produced the first volume of *The Naval War of 1812: A Documentary History.* This series, projected to run to three volumes, promises to provide a parallel source to the Wood volumes by supplying well-edited and reliable texts of the most important United States papers and to become an invaluable resource for scholars of the day after tomorrow.

When one flies at 25,000 feet the world below goes by terribly fast; many an interesting cove or woodsy grove is entirely lost to view. To recapitulate 175 years of United States writing about the Battle of Lake Erie in a brief essay is necessarily an exercise in cruel injustice. Even as the historian measures and assesses, new entrants in the field add their contributions to the mountain of scholarship.[4] Injustice or no, there is one judgment this historian cannot avoid. Until recently United States writing on the War of 1812 has not equaled in quality the best Canadian work. No American scholar of the stature, insight, and imagination of C. P. Stacey has yet produced major work on the war along the northern frontier. The best books on the War of 1812 on the lakes frontier are yet to be written and published—perhaps by historians of this generation.

STUART SUTHERLAND

Canadian Archival Sources and the War of 1812

There are many sources in Canada of a public and private nature that relate to the War of 1812, but they are by no means all of those which are important to the Canadian side of the war. Most Canadian records of the war are really British ones and while there are a lot of sources in Canada which have come from Britain, there are many more still across the ocean, especially genealogical ones, and probably more that remain unknown.

Fortunately, there are a number of detailed inventories to several archives, a list of which is appended to this essay. These guides are, or should be, at most major city and university libraries in Canada, and they are probably in several locations in the border states as well.

The War of 1812 researcher must go to Ottawa to make real progress. The single best place for archival sources in Canada is the National Archives of Canada (NAC), formerly the Public Archives of Canada, on Wellington Street. The NAC is quite easy to use and the majority of the sources is readily available on self-service microfilm reels. The NAC also has the advantage of being open twenty-four hours a day, 365 days a year—so if you find yourself with time on your hands at three o'clock A.M. on Christmas morning, you can always read microfilm.

The NAC recognizes two divisions for manuscript sources: the record groups, or RG, which deal with Canadian government records; and the manuscript groups, or MG, which cover personal papers and copied British government records. In the RGs, the most important group is RG 8, the records of the British military in Canada, generally from the 1790s to the 1890s. The papers were acquired when the dominion archivist persuaded the British government to let them remain when the last British troops left this country early in the century.

To quote an inventory of the group, included in the approximately two thousand volumes are "memoranda, reports, returns, memorials, petitions, certificates, accounts, estimates, claims, general orders, proceedings of boards, instructions and warrants," or in other words, just about everything possible. The major concentration of war-related volumes is in what is termed the C series. This series is organized on a subject basis; that is, a group of volumes will contain material on the commissariat, the Provincial Marine, court-martials, and so on. It has been fully microfilmed and most volumes have an index of names, places, and regiments. There is a partial card index, both on microfilm and in the original, but it does not cover many important volumes and thus is not very useful.

Though two thousand volumes sounds like a daunting figure, only about one-tenth of these have references to the war and only about fifty or so of the latter are completely devoted to it. The major volumes are, not surprisingly, those labeled War 1812, and these are 676 to 688 and, to a lesser extent, 688A to 688E. In the first group are letters from British army and navy officers (most of high rank but many of lower), letters from local officials, returns, general orders, memos, and various miscellaneous documents. They provide, if you will excuse the pun, a blow-by-blow description of the war, and many researchers use them as the main source for the conflict. Of nearly equal importance are the volumes which cover the letter books of the military secretary, or in other words the letters to and from the army headquarters in British North America. These volumes, 1218 to 1227, are arranged chronologically and are unindexed. They give a detailed daily account of military concerns. Last in the first group of papers are the general orders. There are several series (for instance, volumes 1169 to 1172), and they give a backup to the letter books as a means of seeing words turned into actions.

The second level in the C series is the subject volumes. These have a varying number of wartime references and they have not been well treated in the card index, so they will require some searching. For instance, if one were interested in the position of Amherstburg during the war, the series on posts and barracks, military posts, commissariat, transport, medical, Provincial Marine, and those of the regiments stationed there would have to be consulted, and there would be no guarantee that all references would be found. Another problem, and one which also occurs in the first group of papers, is that there are a considerable number of duplicate letters, returns, and the like. The true C series veteran can, therefore, be recognized by the muttering of "I'm sure I've seen that reference somewhere before." There is, nevertheless, a vast amount of useful material in these volumes, and much work remains to be done on them.

Bearing in mind the limitations of the C series, it can be very helpful to genealogists. In my work on British officers of the War of 1812, I have found that the volumes on memorials (19 to 26), half pay (187 to 222), pensioners (187 to 222, and 496 to 504), and petitions for relief (505 to 510) have been of the greatest use. When using these volumes, one should keep in mind that many persons were writing well after the war was over; the volumes mentioned go up to 1870 in some instances.

Besides RG 8, there are a number of other series of importance for specific topics. RG 1 (the records of the Executive Councils for Lower and Upper Canada—i.e., the equivalent of the U.S. Senate), RG 4 (the correspondence of the civil and provincial secretaries for Lower Canada), RG 5 (the same for Upper Canada), RG 7 (records of the governor-general's office), RG 9 (the records of the department of militia and defence), and RG 10 (the records of the Indian Department) are all of use. RG 4 and RG 5 are important for the daily government of the provinces, and of great value here is what is termed the Upper Canada sundries in RG 5, which give very detailed information on civil affairs during the war. The militia records in RG 9 are of course extremely valuable, the more so since there are very few such records in RG 8. Here there is much detailed information on militia muster rolls, officers, general orders, and correspondence, which makes RG 9 particularly helpful to genealogists. All these record groups have a number of finding aids of fairly recent provenance but the National Archives holds manuscript guides, and it is better to consult these first.

Turning to the manuscript groups, the most important series for British official documents are MG 11 (the Colonial Office records), MG 12 (the Admiralty records), and MG 13 (the War Office records); there are also small groups of Foreign Office and Treasury records, but these are of use only peripherally. All these records have been microfilmed from the originals at the Public Record Office in Britain and are of varying scope and usefulness. The Colonial Office papers are the most important in Canada for the military-political overview of the war from the Canadian side. Of the many volumes in the series, the best are those that deal with what is termed "original correspondence" from the governors of the colonies. These contain regular reports from governors to the colonial secretary. Since the war dominated the correspondence, since the colonial secretary was also the secretary of state for war, and since nearly all governors were serving officers, there is much military and naval information as well. Also in the correspondence are many supporting documents from other persons as well as some memorials, petitions, and similar materials. The Lower Canadian volumes are the most important because Governor Sir George Prevost was also the British army commander in chief, and these are CO 42/147 to CO 42/165. Those for Upper Canada are less important, and are CO 42/352 to CO 42/356. Nova Scotia (and Cape Breton, which at this time was a separate colony) is covered in CO 217/89 to CO 217/97, and Newfoundland in CO 194/52 to CO 194/56. There are also series of volumes that give the Colonial Office correspondence to the governors and others that give the acts and journals of the local legislatures.

Essential for an overview of the naval war from the Canadian side, the Admiralty 1 series of the Admiralty papers is the most important. There are some eighty-eight hundred volumes of papers in Admiralty 1, and again it is a relief to be able to say that only volumes 477 to 478, 502, and 509 are the major ones to be consulted. These volumes come from the group known as admirals' correspondence, which are letters the commanders in chief on the various stations sent regularly to the secretary of the Admiralty in London. There is a wealth of information on how the war was going, and there are also miscellaneous supporting documents that can prove useful. They are the best source in Canada for peripheral operations such as the eastern Maine and Chesapeake campaigns, especially since RG 8 devotes comparatively little space to the Maritimes. Next in importance are the captains' letters, whose volumes are filed by letter and then chronologically. The volumes that contain the letters of Sir James Lucas Yeo, commander on the lakes, are 2736 to 2738, and they are doubly important because they have many enclosures of letters from Robert Heriot Barclay. The captains' letters supplement the admirals' letters well, and they sometimes contain muster rolls, appointments, and the like. One final volume in Admiralty 1 might be mentioned, and this is 5445, the records of the Barclay court-martial, which runs to about one hundred pages or so.

The remaining Admiralty records at the National Archives of use for the war are Admiralty 2 and Admiralty 106. In the first, in volumes 930 and 932 to 933, are letters from the secretary of the Admiralty to the commanders in chief abroad; and in the second are the records of the Navy Board, the administrative arm of the Royal Navy. A small selection deals with records of the Halifax dockyard during the war. Unfortunately, neither the Colonial Office nor the Admiralty records contain much genealogical material.

The last major group of British records is the War Office (WO) papers. Since RG 8 deals with the major matters in the army operations, the bulk of the War Office material is important mainly for sidelights, and is particularly helpful for genealogists. The muster books and pay lists for several regiments are available, as are the casualty returns. Also very important, and fairly recently acquired, are the description and succession books, on 107 reels of microfilm, that give a detailed account of the men in each regiment. The WO 17 series of monthly returns for the British North America command is of course essential to an overview of the British army during the war, and there is also much information about officers in these volumes, which are WO 17/1516 to WO 17/1519 for the Canadas and WO 17/2359 to WO 17/2362 for the Nova Scotia command. The general orders in the WO 28 series duplicate those in the RG 8 series to some extent, but the artillery and engineer papers in the WO 44 and WO 55 series should be reviewed since both arms were separate from the rest of the army at this period.

As for the personal papers at the National Archives, the majority is not very extensive for wartime activities, although an exception must be made for the records of Sir John Coape Sherbrooke in MG 24, A57, since Sherbrooke was the commander in chief in the Atlantic provinces and his papers add a good amount of supplementary information to the main collections. There are, in addition, a variety of smaller collections useful for political events—those of H. W. Ryland, J. B. Robinson, and Sir James Stuart, for example—and some for minor military matters, such as the Merritt papers and the David Wingfield papers.

Outside the National Archives, the provincial archives in the eastern provinces contain a variety of material relating to the war. A good example is the Archives of Ontario, or AO, at Toronto. The AO has microfilm copies of most of the RG 8 papers (not, unfortunately, the general orders) and of the CO 42 papers that relate to Upper Canada, as well as a large number of personal collections of many prominent residents, such as John Strachan, the Cartwright family of Kingston, William Dickson of Niagara, and the Jarvis-Powell families of York. A collection of military records is quite extensive, over twenty-five feet worth, but only selected parts relate to the war. There is of course much material of genealogical interest in all these papers, but some digging will be required and, therefore, the major collections at the National Archives should be consulted first. The other major provincial archives with wartime papers is the Archives Nationales du Québec, but it does not publish a catalog and there is no comprehensive list of its holdings. The Public Archives of Nova Scotia in Halifax has a wide variety of papers, the most significant being those in RG 1, the records of the lieutenant governor's office, which really has a much wider scope than is suggested by the name and contains all sorts of material. The militia papers in RG 22 are less useful; some years ago the provincial archivist remarked to me that she could never find anything she wanted in them. However, the records of the Nova Scotia army command are valuable, especially because of the manuscript general orders of this command. The Public Archives of New Brunswick in Fredericton and the Public Archives of Newfoundland and Labrador in St. John's also have much local material which may be of use depending on the scope of one's work.

British-based sources for the war are quite extensive. The single most important repository is, of course, the Public Record Office (PRO) in London, where originals of all the papers of the British government are kept. The amount and scope of the documents is vast—there are, for example, some thirteen thousand volumes in one War Office series alone—and very many are essential for an understanding of the war from the Canadian side. The WO 10 muster rolls, the WO 12 muster rolls, the regimental monthly returns in WO 17, the Admiralty 37 ships' muster rolls, and the WO 25 casualty returns are all very important, especially since very few of them are available in Canada. Naturally, the PRO papers are the best source for the Washington and New Orleans campaign, and the Colonial Office papers on Bermuda are also useful, since Bermuda was in the British North American command during this period. Some series have fairly detailed inventories, and these will normally be found in university or large city libraries.

Useful Archival Guides for Canadian Sources

Craig, Barbara L. and Richard W. Ramsey, compilers. *A Guide to the Holdings of the Archives of Ontario.* 2 vols. Toronto: Ontario Ministry of Citizenship and Culture, 1985.

Cruikshank, E. A., compiler. *Inventory of the Military Documents in the Canadian Archives.* Ottawa: Government Printing Bureau, 1910. [The first inventory of the papers in the present Record Group 8, I, C series papers at the National Archives; somewhat outdated, but a reasonable guide to the contents of the volumes.]

Guide to the Contents of the Public Record Office. 3 vols. London: H. M. Stationery Office, 1963–68. [Volume 2 is the most helpful.]

Inventory of Manuscripts in the Public Archives of Nova Scotia. Halifax: The Archives, 1976.

Public Archives of Canada, Manuscript Division. *General Inventory, Manuscripts*. Vol. 2, *Manuscript Group 11-Manuscript Group 16*. Ottawa: Manuscript Division, 1976. [Contains the main British government papers such as those from the Admiralty, Colonial Office, War Office, Treasury and Foreign Office copied for the archives.]

———. *General Inventory, Manuscripts*. Vol. 4, *Manuscript Group 22-Manuscript Group 25*. Ottawa: Manuscript Division, 1976. [Personal papers of government officials, businessmen, soldiers, and others in the early nineteenth century.]

DOUGLAS E. CLANIN

United States Manuscript Sources for a Study of the War of 1812 in the Northwest

The 175th anniversary of the victory of Commodore Oliver H. Perry and the United States fleet over Captain Robert H. Barclay and the British fleet on Lake Erie on September 10, 1813, provides an excellent opportunity to reconsider not only the significance of that critical naval battle in the War of 1812 but also important elements in the entire history of that conflict. In the United States, Great Britain, and Canada, the events of 1812–15 are beginning to receive more attention, which is indeed to be welcomed since it is a period in the history of all three countries that has often received little notice. In 1969 Professor Reginald Horsman wrote the following accurate observation in his *War of 1812:* "In the twentieth century there has been little interest in the War of 1812 in Britain, and even in the United States far more detailed work has been written on the causes of the war than on the war itself."[1] He went on to list only two general accounts on the war: J. Mackay Hitsman's *The Incredible War of 1812* (1965), written from a Canadian point of view, and Harry Coles, *The War of 1812* (1965), a solid work that was based largely on primary printed sources and secondary accounts.[2] By contrast, Professor Horsman's own work was based not only on secondary accounts and primary printed sources but also on primary research in the British Public Record Office and in the United States National Archives.

Since the publication of Professor Horsman's book in 1969, some noteworthy books of interest to the student of the War of 1812 have made their appearance. John C. Fredriksen's *Resource Guide for the War of 1812* is a useful compilation of primary and secondary printed books and articles.[3] Fredriksen also lists 108 manuscript repositories in his *Guide,* although he only briefly mentions some of their collections and covers the war from a national, rather than a regional, viewpoint.

Canadian author Pierre Berton published two well-received volumes in the early 1980s: *The Invasion of Canada, 1812–1813* and *Flames Across the Border: The Canadian-American Tragedy, 1813–1814*.[4] Both volumes show evidence that Berton made extensive use of primary and secondary sources. However, some readers might object to novelist Berton's interjection of dialogue he creates for some of the characters in his War of 1812 drama. Nevertheless, the author's technique and style of writing does infuse some new life into an old story.

By contrast, a work published in 1983 broke new ground in the realm of traditional scholarship when J. C. A. Stagg's *Mr. Madison's War: Politics, Diplomacy, and Warfare in the Early American Republic, 1783–1830* made its appearance.[5] Stagg utilized not only the standard sources that Horsman had used in his 1969 work, but he also examined some record groups in the United States National Archives that are often overlooked, such as the records of the adjutant generals of the U.S. Army. Despite some limitations, Stagg's book is still a very important work because of the light it sheds on the conduct of the war—particularly James Madison's conduct of that war.

Also in 1983, publishing firm Chadwyck-Healey launched an ambitious project that all researchers are welcoming, despite the unwieldy title of *National Inventory of Documentary Sources in the United States* (NID). Part 1: *Federal Records;* part 2: *Manuscript Division, Library of Congress;* part 3: *State Archives, Libraries, and Historical Societies;* part 4: *Academic Libraries and Other Repositories.* There are two hundred institutions contributing to NID, contrasted with over thirteen hundred repositories that are submitting collection information to the *National Union Catalog of Manuscript Collections* (NUCMC). A principal difference between NID and NUCMC is that collections in NID are described in much more detail than NUCMC because NID reproduces finding aids, indices, and container lists provided by the contributing institutions. Parts 1 and 2 of the Chadwyck-Healey enterprise are now complete and will be updated periodically in the future. Parts 3 and 4 will not be completed in the foreseeable future because the task is enormous.

The appearance of Chadwyck-Healey's NID has also been matched by the appearance of more and more finding aids for major manuscript repositories holding War of 1812 materials. For example, over half of the finding aids used in the preparation of this manuscript bibliography were published after Professor Horsman's *War of 1812.*

Another useful trend that all scholars must welcome is the microfilming of many collections and record groups. This makes increasing numbers of collections available through interlibrary loan or direct purchase by interested persons and institutions. Certainly, any researcher on a tight budget (and aren't most of us in that category?) will welcome any method that will bring copies of materials to him or her rather than having to face long and costly trips to many repositories around the United States or elsewhere.

The U.S. National Archives continues to microfilm much of the older material it holds. In fact, many of the really important subseries that are essential for a study of the War of 1812 in the Northwest have been available for purchase or consultation for many years. The National Archives is currently embarked on a long-range project to microfilm all the loose papers and eventually all the bound volumes of materials of the first twenty or thirty Congresses. Eventually, all the papers of the Congresses that sat during the War of 1812 will be available on microfilm.

The Library of Congress also continues to microfilm its major holdings. The papers of the presidents, including James Madison, James Monroe, and William Henry Harrison, have been available on film for several years. Many of the projects sponsored by the National Historical Publications and Records Commission have also been microfilmed. The Henry Clay Papers and the Albert Gallatin Papers are two of the projects that come to mind but there are also many others. The NHPRC has published a catalog of its microfilm projects that is available from the NHPRC offices in the National Archives Building, Washington, D.C.

Outside of Washington, other state and local repositories are also microfilming or have microfilmed important collections. The Kentucky Historical Society has had its manuscript and newspaper holdings available on microfilm for many years. The Ohio Historical Society sponsored a project over a decade ago to microfilm the papers of thirteen major early Ohio political leaders, including those of Return J. Meigs, Jr., and Thomas Worthington. The State Historical Society of Wisconsin has microfilmed the important Draper Manuscripts twice since World War II. The second filming and the guide to the manuscripts that was published in 1983 certainly make that collection more accessible and useful. The Indiana Historical Society may soon join the ranks of institutions that are microfilming collections. A feasibility study is underway to consider the microfilming of the most heavily used collections, including some of interest to students of the War of 1812: the William Henry Harrison Papers, the William H. English Collection, and the Arthur Mitten Papers.

There are several reasons why repositories are beginning to or already have microfilmed their important collections. Security reasons come first. Many of the documents are not only historically important but are also valuable commodities in the auction market. Second, while the paper and ink in many of the War of 1812 documents have survived remarkably well in many cases, the documents are not indestructible. There is deterioration in each old document every time a xerox print is made from it, every time it is handled, and every time it is exposed to light, humidity, and heat. All of these factors have a deleterious impact on old documents and makes microfilming the originals and retiring them to climate-controlled vaults a very important step toward their long-term preservation and the perpetuation of our past. With the technological advances that are certain to come in the future, documents will become more accessible to greater numbers of people.

The manuscript bibliography that follows this overview is an attempt to compile a list of as many collections as possible that do or may contain documents on the War of 1812 in the Northwest. No special attempt has been made to determine which collections are available on microfilm, with the exception of the U.S. National Archives. The reason for this omission is that some repositories do not loan out their microfilmed collections, some loan but do not offer for sale their microfilmed collections, and some repositories filmed their collections long ago and, in many cases, the only available sets are housed in the parent repositories, or are no longer available for sale. Conversely, some newly microfilmed collections may just now be available. Researchers should always check with the manuscript curator of each institution of interest to learn of the availability of their collections on microfilm.

What follows is a short survey of some important collections and record groups in some key repositories. This does not mean to imply that other collections or record groups, by their omission, are not important; on the contrary, they often contain documents of extreme importance for anyone conducting research on War of 1812 topics. However, the collections mentioned do contain a rich lode of War of 1812 materials that could be mined with profit by anyone interested in this historical period.

Since Horsman's *War of 1812* was published in 1969, some things have not changed. The observations he makes in his bibliographical note to that work are still valid: A good place for anyone to start when beginning research on the War of 1812 is the U.S. National Archives.[6]

Following Horsman's lead, the most important record groups in the National Archives for a study of the War of 1812 in the Northwest are RG 107: Records of the Office of the Secretary of War, and RG 45: Naval Records Collection of the Office of Naval Records and Library. In RG 107, microfilm publications M6, M22, M221, and M222 are very important, although, as Horsman notes, these record series contain many serious gaps, and they need to be supplemented with other sources.

In RG 45, microfilm publications M147 and M149 (probably among others) have letters to and from Oliver H. Perry; Isaac Chauncey; William Jones, the secretary of the navy in 1813; and a host of other naval figures. The publication of the remaining volumes of *The Naval War of 1812: A Documentary History,* edited by William S. Dudley and others, will open up new vistas for many scholars to other naval records in the National Archives.

One final record group at the National Archives that should be mentioned is RG 94: Records of the Adjutant General's Office, 1780s–1917. It contains a large mass of material, much of it poorly organized, but RG 94 is a record group not to be overlooked.

In the Library of Congress's Manuscript Division, housed in the relatively new James Madison Building, are numerous important collections, including the James Madison Papers, the William Henry Harrison Papers, and the Duncan McArthur Papers. The first two of these are readily available on microfilm, and the Ohio Historical Society has a complete set of the McArthur Papers on film.

Many states make accessible worthwhile collections of War of 1812 materials. Starting with Indiana repositories, the Lilly Library at Indiana University, Bloomington, has a large collection of War of 1812 documents. It is also blessed with a fine card catalog indexing this material. In Indianapolis, the Indiana Division of the Indiana State Library houses two important collections: the Lasselle Family Papers and the John Tipton Papers. Also in Indianapolis is the Indiana Historical Society, which has an important collection of William Henry Harrison Papers as well as rich and varied autograph collections assembled by William H. English and Arthur Mitten.

In Frankfort, Kentucky, the Kentucky Historical Society has a large number of collections on the War of 1812, but the grand total is smaller than for some repositories. A definite plus for researchers is the availability of this material on microfilm. On a larger scale than the Kentucky Historical Society, but still somewhat smaller in total bulk than other repositories, is the Filson Club in Louisville, but it is still an important collection.

Traveling north to Michigan, one must make a stop at the William L. Clements Library at the University of Michigan, Ann Arbor. Their Oliver H. Perry Collection is the largest in the United States outside of the National Archives.

The Burton Historical Collection, housed in the Detroit Public Library, contains probably the largest and most varied collection of War of 1812 materials outside of Washington, D.C. A researcher could spend many profitable days searching the vast Burton holdings.

Heading east to New York City, one can find small but important collections housed in two major repositories: the New-York Historical Society and the New York Public Library.

Again in the Midwest, the Cincinnati Historical Society contains numerous important collections worth special notice, including the John S. Gano Papers, the various William Henry Harrison collections, the Aaron Torrence Collection, the Robert Clarke Papers, and various miscellaneous files of documents that are worth examining at length.

Moving north to the Western Reserve Historical Society in Cleveland, one finds an excellent War of 1812 collection consisting of the Elijah Wadsworth Papers and the Simon Perkins Papers—a collection rich in War of 1812 manuscripts.

The Ohio Historical Society in Columbus is loaded with important collections, many of which are available on microfilm. One outstanding collection is the papers of Return J. Meigs, Jr.

Traveling back east, one must stop at the Historical Society of Pennsylvania in Philadelphia. There are many important autograph collections housed here, but a researcher should not overlook the William Jones Papers and the Daniel Parker Papers.

Located southwest of Philadelphia is the Tennessee State Library and Archives in Nashville, which houses not only its own collection of James Winchester Papers but also a collection of Winchester papers that belongs to the Tennessee Historical Society. All of the Winchester manuscripts have been microfilmed and are probably still available for purchase.

The final stop on this fast-paced tour of manuscript repositories and collections is probably made at the granddaddy of the major collections of War of 1812 materials outside of Washington: the Draper Manuscripts (on film) in Madison, Wisconsin. There is only a semblance of an organization to the Draper Manuscripts, but what an invaluable resource for the study of the United States and Canada, especially the frontier areas, down to 1815!

Compiled by DOUGLAS E. CLANIN

A Bibliography of United States Manuscript Sources for a Study of the War of 1812 in the Northwest

The following bibliography is the culmination of an effort to bring together in one list many major and minor collections and individual items that would prove useful to anyone conducting research into aspects of the War of 1812 in the Northwest, a geographical region that I have rather arbitrarily defined as the Great Lakes area from the Niagara frontier to the Mississippi Valley and northward from Kentucky and the Ohio Valley to the Canadian border.

Every attempt has been made to insure the completeness of this listing, but perhaps no bibliography of this type can ever be considered definitive. Various institutions around the United States add relevant collections to their holdings from time to time and some institutions or collections may have been inadvertently overlooked during the preparation of this bibliography. For example in some repositories, collections of miscellaneous manuscripts, which are sometimes uncataloged, can often be searched with profit. Thus, the interested reader should look upon this listing as an interim report, one that will need to be revised from time to time.

The bulk of this bibliography was prepared from listing sheets and control files collected by me and other staff members of the Indiana Historical Society in the research phase of the preparation of a microfilm edition of the papers of William Henry Harrison, 1800–1815. In the course of this research, contact was made with over one thousand repositories across the United States, Canada, and Great Britain. In addition, over thirty repositories were visited in eight states and the District of Columbia in an effort to collect all relevant documents written by or sent to William Henry Harrison from 1800 to 1815.

To supplement the Harrison search material, the following national and individual repository manuscript guides and repository directories were also consulted:

National

American Library Directory, 1987–88, 40th ed., 2 vols. (New York and London: R. R. Bowker Co., 1987); Philip M. Hamer, ed., *A Guide to Archives and Manuscripts in the United States* (New Haven, CT: Yale University Press, 1961); Library of Congress, *The National Union Catalog of Manuscript Collections, 1959–* (Ann Arbor, MI, and elsewhere: J. W. Edwards and others, 1962-); National Historical Publications and Records Commission, *Directory of Archives and Manuscript Repositories in the United States* (Washington, D.C.: National Archives and Records Service/General Services Administration, 1978); and Betty Pease Smith, comp. and ed., *Directory* [of] *Historical Agencies in North America;* 13th ed. (Nashville, TN: American Association for State and Local History, 1986); *Guide to the National Archives of the United States* (Washington, D.C.: National Archives and Records Service/General Services Administration, 1974); and National Archives, *Microfilm Resources for Research: A Comprehensive Catalog* (Washington, D.C.: National Archives and Records Administration, 1986).

States

CALIFORNIA: *Guide to American Historical Manuscripts in the Huntington Library* (San Marino, CA: Huntington Library, 1979).

ILLINOIS: Maynard J. Brickford et al., *Manuscripts Guide to Collections at the University of Illinois at Urbana-Champaign* (Urbana: University of Illinois Press, 1976).

INDIANA: Eric Pumroy, with Paul Brockman, *A Guide to Manuscript Collections of the Indiana Historical Society and Indiana State Library* (Indianapolis: Indiana Historical Society, 1986).

IOWA: Katherine Harris, comp., *Guide to Manuscripts* [in the State Historical Society of Iowa] (Iowa City: State Historical Society of Iowa, 1973).

KENTUCKY: Joan Brookes-Smith, ed., *Kentucky Historical Society Microfilm Catalog,* 2 vols. (Frankfort, KY: Kentucky Historical Society, 1975); and G. Glenn Clift, *Guide to the Manuscripts of the Kentucky Historical Society* (Frankfort, KY: Kentucky Historical Society, 1955).

MARYLAND: Avril J. M. Pedley, comp., *The Manuscript Collections of the Maryland Historical Society* (Baltimore: Maryland Historical Society, 1968).

MICHIGAN: William S. Ewing, comp., *Guide to the Manuscript Collections in the William L. Clements Library* (Ann Arbor, MI: Clements Library, 1953); Thomas E. Powers and William H. McNitt, *Guide to Manuscripts in the Bentley Historical Library* (Ann Arbor: University of Michigan, 1976); and Bernice Cox Sprenger, comp., *Guide to the Manuscripts in the Burton Historical Collection* (Detroit: Burton Historical Collection, Detroit Public Library, 1985).

MINNESOTA: Lucile M. Kane and Kathryn A. Johnson, comps., *Manuscript Collections of the Minnesota Historical Society, Guide Number 2* (St. Paul: Minnesota Historical Society, 1955); and Grace Lee Nute and Gertrude W. Ackermann, comps., *Guide to the Personal Papers in the Manuscript Collections of the Minnesota Historical Society* (St. Paul: Minnesota Historical Society, 1935).

NORTH CAROLINA: Richard C. Davis et al., eds., *Guide to the Catalogued Collections in the Manuscript Department of the William R. Perkins Library, Duke University* (Santa Barbara, CA, and Oxford, Eng.: Clio Books, 1980).

OHIO: Linda Elise Kalette, comp. and ed., *The Papers of Thirteen Early Ohio Political Leaders . . . : An Inventory to the 1976–77 Microfilm Editions* (Columbus: Ohio Historical Society, 1977); and Andrea D. Lentz and Sara S. Fuller, eds., *A Guide to Manuscripts at the Ohio Historical Society* (Columbus: Ohio Historical Society, 1972).

WISCONSIN: Josephine L. Harper, *Guide to the Draper Manuscripts* (Madison: State Historical Society of Wisconsin, 1983).

Entries were also collected from John C. Fredriksen's *Resource Guide for the War of 1812.* Many thanks to Mr. Fredriksen for granting permission to use materials from his *Resource Guide.*

Symbols appearing in this manuscript bibliography are as follows: An asterisk (*) is used preceding the name of a collection or microfilm series if it contains one or more items that relate to the War of 1812 in the Northwest. Other collections (not preceded by an asterisk) are included in this listing because, although no relevant documents could be found in them, either based on actual research in the collections or on information contained in various manuscript guides, on closer examination some relevant documents might be discovered in the collections. The manuscript curator at each repository listed will be able to provide additional information about these unasterisked collections.

In the National Archives portion of the bibliography, "RG" stands for the Record Group, and "M" and "T," letters which precede numbers in the listing, are microfilm series designations. Throughout the listing, the letters "WHH" stand for William Henry Harrison. For some repositories, only one or two Harrison documents of War of 1812 date were found. However, as mentioned above, there could be other relevant documents in those same repositories.

Because of the narrow focus of the following bibliography and in the interest of saving space, all references to complete date ranges and total size of complete collections or the specific number of reels of microfilm in each large series have been deleted. However, if a specific collection covers just the War of 1812, more detailed information has been supplied.

National

Library of Congress:

*Louis Eller Asher Autograph Collection; *Journal of Major Lewis Bond, June 29, 1812–May 1813 (1 vol.); *Breckinridge Family Papers; *Jacob Jennings Brown Papers; *Lewis Cass Folder, Miscellaneous Manuscripts Collection; *Henry Clay Papers; *Clay Family Papers; William Harris Crawford Papers; *John Jordan Crittenden Papers; *George Croghan Papers; Papers of Joseph and John R. Desha; Edward Lee Dorsett Collection in the Naval Historical Foundation Collection; *Ewing Family Papers; Albert Gallatin Papers; *William Henry Harrison Papers; *Thomas Sidney Jesup Papers; Richard Mentor Johnson Papers; Jacob Kingsbury Papers; *Duncan McArthur Papers; *James Madison Papers; *Return Jonathan Meigs, Jr., Papers, Miscellaneous Manuscripts Collection; *Michigan Territory Folder, Miscellaneous Manuscripts Collection; *James Monroe Papers; *James Morrison Business Correspondence; *John Payne Papers; *John H. Piatt Letter Book, 1812–1813 (1 vol.), Miscellaneous Manuscripts Collection; *Shelby Family Papers; *Short, Harrison, and Symmes Families Papers; *Stevens Family Papers; James Wilkinson Papers; *Thomas Worthington Diaries, September 19, 1811–June 8, 1815 (6 vols.), Miscellaneous Manuscripts Collection; *Thomas Worthington Papers

National Archives:

RG 24: Records of the Bureau of Naval Personnel

RG 45: Naval Records Collection of the Office of Naval Records and Library

M124 Letters Received by the Secretary of the Navy: Miscellaneous Letters
M125 Letters Received by the Secretary of the Navy: Captains' Letters
*M147 Letters Received by the Secretary of the Navy from Commanders
M148 Letters Received by the Secretary of the Navy from Officers below the Rank of Commander
*M149 Letters Sent by the Secretary of the Navy to Officers
M209 Miscellaneous Letters Sent by the Secretary of the Navy
M441 Letters Sent by the Secretary of the Navy to Commanders and Navy Agents

RG 46: Records of the United States Senate

*Loose papers and bound volumes of the 12th–14th Congresses, 1811–1817
M200 Territorial Papers of the United States Senate
M1251 Journals of the Legislative Proceedings of the United States Senate

RG 52: Records of the Bureau of Medicine and Surgery, United States Navy

RG 59: General Records of the Department of State

M40 Domestic Letters of the Department of State
*M179 Miscellaneous Letters of the Department of State
*M588 "War of 1812 Papers" of the Department of State, 1789–1815
M1134 State Department Territorial Papers, Missouri

RG 75: Records of the Bureau of Indian Affairs

M1 Records of the Michigan Superintendency of Indian Affairs
M15 Letters Sent by the Secretary of War Relating to Indian Affairs
M16 Letters Sent by the Superintendent of Indian Trade
M271 Letters Received by the Office of the Secretary of War Relating to Indian Affairs

M574 Special Files of the Office of Indian Affairs
T58 Letters Received by the Superintendent of Indian Trade

RG 77: Records of the Office of the Chief of Engineers, United States Army

M417 Buell Collection of Historical Documents Relating to the Corps of Engineers
M1113 Letters Sent by the Chief of Engineers

RG 80: General Records of the Department of the Navy

*RG 92: Records of the Office of the Quartermaster General, United States Army

RG 94: Records of the Adjutant General's Office, 1780s–1917, United States Army

*Miscellaneous document files
*M565 Letters Sent by the Office of the Adjutant General, Main Series
*M566 Letters Received by the Office of the Adjutant General
M617 Returns from United States Military Posts
M661 Historical Information Relating to Military Posts and Other Installations
*M711 Registers of Letters Received, Office of the Adjutant General
*M1094 General Orders and Circulars of the War Department and Headquarters of the Army
T1085 Muster Rolls and Payrolls of Militia and Regular Army Organizations in the Battle of Tippecanoe, November 1811

RG 98: Records of United States Army Commands

*RG 99: Records of the Office of the Paymaster General, United States Army

RG 107: Records of the Office of the Secretary of War

*M6 Letters Sent by the Secretary of War Relating to Military Affairs
*M7 Confidential and Unofficial Letters Sent by the Secretary of War
*M22 Registers of Letters Received by the Office of the Secretary of War, Main Series
*M127 Letters Sent to the President by the Secretary of War
*M220 Reports to Congress from the Secretary of War
*M221 Letters Received by the Secretary of War, Registered Series
*M222 Letters Received by the Secretary of War, Unregistered Series

RG 112: Records of the Office of the Surgeon General, United States Army

RG 125: Records of the Office of the Judge Advocate General, United States Navy

RG 127: Records of the United States Marine Corps, United States Navy

RG 153: Records of the Office of the Judge Advocate General, United States Army

M1105 Registers of the Records of the Proceedings of the United States Army General Courts-Martial

RG 156: Records of the Office of the Chief of Ordnance, United States Navy

RG 159: Records of the Office of the Inspector General, United States Army

M624 Inspection Reports of the Office of the Inspector General

RG 192: Records of the Office of the Commissary General of Subsistence, United States Army

RG 203: Records of the Office of the Chief of Finance, United States Army

RG 233: Records of the United States House of Representatives

*Loose papers and bound volumes of the 12th–14th Congresses, 1811–1817

National Society of the Daughters of the American Revolution, National Headquarters:

*one WHH document

Naval Historical Foundation, Washington Navy Yard:

*Thomas Holdup Stevens on Jesse Duncan Elliott

States

California

San Marino:

The Huntington Library:
William Henry Allen Correspondence; Lawrence F. Bower Autograph Collection; *Charles T. Harbeck Collection; *William Henry Harrison Papers

Stanford:

Stanford University Library:
*Jesse Duncan Elliott material in the Harwood Family Papers

Connecticut

New Haven:

Yale University Library:
*James R. Butler, "History of the Pittsburgh Blues"; *John Stites Gano Papers; *Park Family Papers; *Pequot Collection; *Stephen Van Rensselaer Letters, 1812 (five items); *Wetmore Family Papers; Joseph Wheaton Papers

Illinois

Bloomington:

McLean County Historical Society:
*Custer Milo Collection

Chicago:

Chicago Historical Society:
*Lewis Cass Collection; *William Clark Papers; *Ninian Edwards Papers; *Hardin Family Papers; *William Henry Harrison Collection; Indians of the Chicago Region Collection; *Andrew Jackson Papers; *Jacob Kingsbury Papers; Pierre Menard Papers; *Oliver H. Perry Papers; *Thomas Todd Collection; *Vincennes Papers; *James Wilkinson Papers
Newberry Library:
*John Howard Payne Papers in the Edward E. Ayer Collection

Joseph Regenstein Library, University of Chicago:
*Reuben Thomas Durrett's Papers on Kentucky and the Ohio River Valley; *William Hayden English Papers; *Miscellaneous Manuscript Collection

Springfield:

Illinois State Archives:
*Papers of the governor, secretary of state, adjutant general, and recognition boards
Illinois State Historical Library:
*Henry S. Dodge Papers; *Ninian Edwards Papers; Pierre Menard Papers; Jesse B. Thomas Papers

Urbana-Champaign:

University of Illinois Library:
*Capt. Joseph Cross's First Regiment of Illinois Artillery Record Book, 1812–1814 (1 vol.); *Charles Knight Correspondence; Pierre Menard Papers

Indiana

Bloomington:

Lilly Library, Indiana University:
*Henry Clay Papers; *William Henry Harrison Collection; *Jackson Manuscripts; *Return J. Meigs, Jr., Papers; *Polke Manuscripts; *U.S. History Manuscripts; *War of 1812 Manuscripts (4,405-plus items); *Jonathan Williams Papers; *Samuel Williams Manuscripts

Fort Wayne:

Allen County-Fort Wayne Historical Society:
*John Kelso Letters; *one WHH document
Louis A. Warren Lincoln Library and Museum:
*Presidential Autographs Collection

Indianapolis:

Commission on Public Records, Indiana State Archives:
*Territorial court and executive records
Indiana Division, Indiana State Library:
Elisha Cox Papers; *William Henry Harrison Papers; *Ephraim Jordan Papers; *Lasselle Family Papers; *John Tipton Papers

Indiana Historical Society:
*J. David Baker Collection; *William Hayden English Collection; *William Henry Harrison Papers; *Indiana Territory Papers; *Arthur G. Mitten Papers; Old Northwest Papers; Elihu Stout Papers; *Samuel C. Vance Papers

Iowa

Iowa City:

State Historical Society of Iowa:
Robert Lucas Papers

Kentucky

Bowling Green:

Helm-Cravens Library, Western Kentucky University:
*John Bibb Account of the River Raisin Massacre; *Isaac Shelby Papers; *Joseph R. Underwood Narrative of the Siege of Fort Meigs, 1813 (transcript)

Frankfort:

Kentucky Department for Libraries and Archives:
*Gov. Charles Scott's Military Papers; *Gov. Isaac Shelby's Letter Books, 1812–1816 (2 vols.); *Gov. Isaac Shelby's Military Papers
Kentucky Historical Society:
*Josiah Bacon Letters; *Thomas Bodley Papers; *William O. Butler Poem about the Battle of the River Raisin, 1813 (1 item); *Green Clay Papers, 1813 (1 item); *Henry Clay Papers; *William Creighton, Sr., Papers; *Capt. Peter Dudley Papers, 1813 (1 vol.); *Sgt. Ennis Duncan Papers, 1814–1815 (13 items); *Capt. James Duncan Papers, 1813 (1 item); *James T. Eubank Letter Book, 1813–1814 (1 vol.); *William Eustis Papers, 1812 (1 item, photostat); *William Henry Harrison Papers; *Paschal Hickman Papers, 1813 (1 item); *Samuel Hopkins Papers; *William Hull Papers, 1812 (2 items); *James Johnson Papers (1 item); *Kentucky Military Records; *Kentucky Militia Miscellaneous Papers; *Kentucky Militia Muster Rolls; *Kentucky Militia Officers Rosters, 1812–1816 (3 vols.); *Philip and Robert Latham Papers, 1813 (1 item); *Maj. William R. McGary Papers, 1813 (1 item); *John McLean Papers, 1815 (1 item); *James Miller Papers, 1815 (1 item); *James Morrison Papers, 1812–1815 (5 items); *William B. Northcutt "Diary" (i.e., Reminiscences); *Robert Scott Papers, 1812 (1 item);

*Maxwell Sharp Papers, 1812 (1 item); *Isaac Shelby Papers; *Samuel Starks Papers, 1814 (1 item); *Capt. James Sympson's Diary, 1813 (1 vol.); *James Taylor Papers; *Charles A. Wickliffe Papers; *James Winchester Papers, 1812 (1 item)

Lexington:

Margaret King Library, University of Kentucky:
*Allen-Butler Family Papers; Henry Clay Papers; Charles Scott Papers; James Shannon Papers; Isaac Shelby and Family Papers; *Hubbard Taylor Papers; *War of 1812 Miscellany (4? items); *Samuel M. Wilson Collection, including copies of a Green Clay Order Book, August–September 1813, and Isaac Shelby Letter Books, 1812–1816; *Edwin Bedford Green Narrative of the War of 1812

Louisville:

Filson Club:
*William Taylor Barry Papers (transcripts only); *William Kennedy Beall Journal, 1812 (1 vol.); Temple Bodley Papers; *Correspondence of Thomas Bodley; *Arthur Lee Campbell Papers; *Isaac Clark Papers; *Green Clay Papers, March-April 1813 (1 item); *William Croghan Family Papers; *Miscellaneous Diaries and Journals; Papers of the Governors of Kentucky; *Gwathmey Family Papers; *Henry Family Papers; *Joyes Family Papers; *William Lewis Order Book, November 19, 1812–February 14, 1813 (1 vol.), in the R. C. Ballard Thruston Collection; *James Young Love Papers; *Robert B. McAfee Papers; *Samuel McDowell Papers; *David Meriwether Memoirs; *John O'Fallon Papers; *Preston Family Papers-Joyes Collection; Isaac Shelby Papers; *Slaughter Family Papers; Papers of James Taylor and James Taylor, Jr.; *Taylor Family Papers; *Edward C. Thurman Collection of Stampless Covers Representing Towns and Cities of Kentucky; *Charles Stewart Todd Papers; Stephen Fitz James Trabue Papers

Maryland

Annapolis:

U.S. Naval Academy Library:
*one Oliver H. Perry letter, 1813

Baltimore:

Maryland Historical Society:
*Samuel Hambleton Diary; Hambleton Family Papers

Massachusetts

Boston:

Boston Public Library:
*Mellen Chamberlain Autograph Collection
Boston University Library:
Edward C. Stone's American Statesmen Collection
Massachusetts Historical Society:
*Jacob Jennings Brown Papers; *Benjamin Hough Account of the Battle of the Thames, 1813; *Miscellaneous Manuscript Collection

Cambridge:

Houghton Library, Harvard University
*William Hull Papers in the James Freeman Clarke Collection

Williamstown:

Chapin Library, Williams College:
*William Henry Harrison Papers

Worcester:

American Antiquarian Society:
*Collection of orderly books, War of 1812 (2 vols.); *Papers Relating to the War of 1812 (1 box)

Michigan

Ann Arbor:

Bentley Historical Library, University of Michigan:
John Anderson Family Papers; *William Baird Expense Account, 1812 (1 item); Military Topics; George Bryan Porter Papers; *River Raisin Monument Commission Records
William L. Clements Library, University of Michigan:
Jacob Jennings Brown Papers; *Lewis Cass Papers; *Isaac Chauncey Letter Books, War of 1812; Croghan Family Papers; *Fort Wayne Indian Agency Letter Book of John Johnston and Benjamin F. Stickney; Thomas Sidney Jesup Papers; *James McHenry Papers; *Michigan Collection; Military Papers; Miscellaneous Manuscripts; *Orderly Book Collection; *Papers Relating to the War of 1812, 1807–1825 (179 items); *Oliver H. Perry Papers; *War of 1812 Collection, 1806–1820 (250 items)

Detroit:

Burton Historical Collection, Detroit Public Library:
John Anderson Letters; *Charles Askin Papers; *John Askin Papers; Caleb Atwater Papers; Reuben Atwater Papers; Peter Audrain Papers; *Levi Bishop Correspondence and Papers; Thomas J. Bishop Papers; *Lewis Bond Correspondence and Papers; John Parker Boyd Orderly Book, 1811–1812 (1 wallet); *Joriah Brady Papers, 1811–1813 (1 wallet); *Henry B. Brevoort Correspondence and Papers; Jacob Brown Correspondence and Papers; *John Burrows Correspondence, 1812–1814 (1 wallet); *Clarence M. Burton Correspondence and Papers; *Anthony Butler Correspondence and Papers; Campau Family Papers; *Lewis Cass Correspondence and Papers; Auguste Chouteau Correspondence and Papers; *Green Clay Correspondence and Papers; *Sgt. Ennis Duncan, Jr., Orderly Book, 1814–1815 (1 wallet of transcripts); *Jesse Duncan Elliott Correspondence; *Charles E. Feinberg Papers; *Otto O. Fisher Correspondence and Papers; *Fort Erie Papers, 1814 (1 wallet); *Stephen C. Foster Correspondence and Papers; Alexander D. Fraser Correspondence and Papers; *John Gibson Papers; *Gabriel J. Godfroy Papers; *Charles Gratiot Correspondence and Papers; *William Henry Harrison Correspondence and Papers; *Nathaniel Hart Papers; *Nathan Heald Correspondence; *Andrew Hunter Holmes Papers, 1814 (1 wallet); *William Hull Correspondence and Papers; *George Hunt Correspondence and Papers, 1813–1814 (1 wallet); Samuel Huntington Papers; George Ironside Correspondence and Papers; *Nehemiah Jones Correspondence, 1812–1813 (1 wallet); *Benjamin B. Kercheval Correspondence and Papers; *Jacob Kingsbury Correspondence and Papers; *John Kinzie Papers; *William Kirby Correspondence and Papers; *Joseph H. Larwill Papers; William F. Lawler Papers; *William Lewis Orderly Book, 1812–1813 (1 wallet, photostat of original in the Filson Club, Louisville); *Benson John Lossing Correspondence and Papers; *Duncan McArthur Correspondence and Papers, 1813–1818 (2 wallets, 4 vols. of photostats from the Library of Congress); *James McCluskey Correspondence and Papers; John McDonell Papers; *Robert McDouall Papers, 1815, Orderly Book of British Garrison on Drummond Island (1 wallet); George McDougall Correspondence and Papers; *Macomb Family Correspondence and Papers; Samuel W. May Papers; *Return J. Meigs, Jr., Correspondence and Papers; Pierre Menard Correspondence and Papers (on microfilm); *John Miller Papers, 1815 (1 wallet); *Miscellany by Date: Correspondence and Papers; *James Monroe Correspondence; George Morell Papers; Francis Navarre Correspondence and

Papers; *Oliver H. Perry Correspondence, 1810–1815 (1 wallet of photostats); *William Pixley Papers, 1812 (1 wallet); *George Prevost Correspondence, 1812 (1 wallet); *Alexander Pringle Correspondence and Papers, 1815 (1 wallet); *Henry Procter Correspondence, 1812 (1 wallet of photostats from the National Archives of Canada, Ottawa); *Milo M. Quaife Correspondence and Papers; *James Rhea Papers; Gabriel Richard Correspondence and Papers; *John Robinson Diary, 1812 (1 wallet of photostats); William M. Scott Papers; *Isaac Shelby Papers, 1813, Orderly Book (1 wallet, transcript); Solomon Sibley Correspondence and Papers; *Arthur Sinclair Papers, 1814 (1 wallet); *Richard Smyth Papers; *James B. Spencer Correspondence, 1815 (1 wallet); Stanton Family Correspondence and Papers; *Record Book of the Superintendent of Indian Affairs in Michigan; *Lawrence Taliaferro Correspondence and Papers; (4 reels of microfilm from the Minnesota Historical Society); *James Taylor Papers; *Biographical Sketch of Tecumseh by John Law (1 wallet); *Edward Tiffin Correspondence and Papers; *U.S. National Archives Collections (transcripts and photocopies); *War of 1812: Sesquicentennial Celebration Committee Correspondence; *Governor's Commission to Observe the Sesquicentennial of the War of 1812, Records; *War of 1812 Collection, "Northwestern Army"; John R. Williams Correspondence and Papers; Williams Family Papers; *James Winchester Papers, 1812–1813, including orderly books (1 box, including photostats); *Benjamin F. H. Witherell Correspondence and Papers: James Witherell Papers; *William Woodbridge Correspondence and Papers; *Augustus Brevoort Woodward Correspondence and Papers; Woolsey Family Papers; *Samuel Zug Correspondence and Papers

Kalamazoo:

Dwight B. Waldo Library, Western Michigan University:
*Sgt. Greenberry [Greenbury Keen?—*see* Historical Society of Western Pennsylvania entry] Journal, 1812–1813 (1 vol.)

Monroe:

Monroe County Historical Commission:
*Laurent Durocher Papers; *Navarre Family Papers

Mount Pleasant:

Clarke Historical Library, Central Michigan University:
*Charles G. Boerstler Papers; *Samuel McCullough Papers; *Military Papers

Minnesota

St. Paul:

Minnesota Historical Society:
*Robert Dickson Papers (1 box of transcripts and photostats from the National Archives of Canada, Ottawa, and the State Historical Society of Wisconsin, Madison); *Allyn K. Ford Collection; *Lawrence Taliaferro Papers

Missouri

St. Louis:

Mercantile Library Association:
Daniel Bissell Papers; St. Louis and Louisiana Territory Papers
Missouri Historical Society:
Edward Bates Papers; Frederick Bates Papers; Daniel Bissell Papers; Chouteau Family Papers; *William Clark Papers; Delassus-St. Vrain Papers; Rufus Easton Papers; *Thomas Forsyth Papers; *Thomas Forsyth Papers in the Tesson Collection; *Richard Graham Papers; Graham Family Papers in the Fordyce Collection; Charles Gratiot Papers; Jacob Kingsbury Papers in the James W. Kingsbury Collection; John B. C. Lucas and James H. Lucas Papers; Alexander McNair Papers; Pierre Menard Papers; Missouri Governors Collection; *John O'Fallon Collection; *Presidents Collection; *Elmire P. Tesson Papers; *Vasquez Papers; *War of 1812 Collection

New Hampshire

Hanover:

Dartmouth College Library:
*one WHH letter

New Jersey

Morristown:

Morristown National Historical Park:
Lloyd W. Smith Papers

New Brunswick:

Rutgers University Library:
John R. Williams Papers

Princeton:

Princeton University Library:
*Andre De Coppet, American Historical Papers; *General Manuscripts Miscellaneous—three Oliver H. Perry letters, 1813

New York

Albany:

Albany Institute of History and Art:
*Papers of Presidents and Vice Presidents of the United States
New York State Library:
Charles Kitchell Gardner Papers; Morgan Lewis Papers; *War of 1812 Records, 1783–1826 (25 vols.)

Buffalo:

Buffalo and Erie County Historical Society:
*Daniel Dobbins Papers; *War of 1812 Collection, 1812–1928 (ca. 135 items); *Peter Buell Porter Papers

Geneva:

Geneva Historical Society:
*Hugh W. Dobbins Papers

Hyde Park:

Franklin D. Roosevelt Library:
Franklin D. Roosevelt Autograph Collection

New York City:

Rare Book and Manuscript Library, Columbia University:
*Special Manuscript Collection-Alexander Hamilton Papers—one WHH letter
Pierpont Morgan Library:
*Jefferson Album—one WHH letter
New-York Historical Society:
*Isaac Chauncey Papers; Chrystie Family Papers; James Fenimore Cooper Papers; *Albert Gallatin Papers; *McBean Collection; *George McFeely Diary; James Madison Papers; *Miscellaneous Manuscripts—"E"—Ninian Edwards Papers; *Miscellaneous Manuscripts—"H"—William H. Harrison Papers; *Miscellaneous Manuscripts—"S"—Isaac Shelby; *Orderly Book of the 25th U.S. Infantry

New York Public Library:
*Green Clay Papers; *George Croghan Papers; *William Henry Harrison Papers; *James Madison Papers; *James Monroe Papers; *Oliver H. Perry Letters, U.S. Navy Collection; Winfield Scott Papers (mostly typed copies)

Newburgh:

Washington's Headquarters and Museum (Jonathan Hasbrouck House):
*Miscellaneous Military Papers, including an 1812 diary of Micah Brooks on the Canadian frontier

Rochester:

University of Rochester Library:
*Nathaniel Rochester Papers Relating to the War of 1812, 1813–1815 (32 items)

Sacket's Harbor:

Pickering-Beach Historical Museum:
*Sacket's Harbor and War of 1812 Collection, 1807–1858

West Point:

U.S. Military Academy Library:
James Miller Papers

North Carolina

Chapel Hill:

University of North Carolina Library-Southern Historical Collection:
Joel Leftwich Papers

Durham:

William R. Perkins Library, Duke University:
*Electus Backus Papers; *Benson Family Papers; *Campbell Family Papers; *Sgt. Ennis Duncan, Jr., Diary, 1814–1815 (1 vol., copy); *John Lang Diary, 1813–1814, British soldier in Canada (1 vol.); John Moore McCalla Papers; Andrew Pinkham Papers

Ohio

Chillicothe:

Ross County Historical Society Museum:
*William Henry Harrison Papers; Duncan McArthur Papers; Edward Tiffin Papers; *Samuel Williams Papers; *Thomas Worthington Papers

Cincinnati:

Cincinnati Historical Society:
*Henry Brown Papers; *Robert Clarke Papers; *Henry Disbraw (or Disbrow) Narrative of the War of 1812; *John Stites Gano Papers; *Gano Family Papers; *James Albert Green Collection of William Henry Harrison Memorabilia; *William Henry Harrison Papers; *Harrison Family Papers; *Joseph H. Hawkins Narrative of the Siege of Fort Meigs; John Johnston Papers; *William Lytle Correspondence; *James McBride Papers; *Miscellaneous Collections of Documents; *Miscellaneous Vertical File; *Reeder Family Papers; *Short Family Papers; Todd Family Papers; *Aaron Torrence Collection

Cleveland:

Western Reserve Historical Society:
*Account of the River Raisin Massacre, January 1813; Quintus F. Atkins Papers; *Lewis Bond Journal, June 29, 1812–February 23, 1813, in Vertical File "B" (copy); *James Bonner Diary, January 1–April 1, 1813, in Vertical File "B"; David Clendenin Papers; Coffinberry Family Papers; *Diary Kept at Upper Sandusky [Ohio] and Fort Meigs, 1812–1814 (1 vol.?); Diaries and Journals; *John Stites Gano Papers; *William Henry Harrison Papers, in Vertical File "H"; John Hayslip Papers; Charles Hegins Papers; Peter and Reuben Hitchcock and Family Papers; *Samuel Huntington Correspondence; *Journal of an Officer of the British Royal Marines, 1813–1814 (1 vol.); Gleason F. Lewis Record Books; *Nathaniel Massie Papers; Military Papers and Records; *Robert Castle Norton Autograph Collection of Letters of the Presidents of the United States; Ohio Militia Records; *Simon Perkins Papers; *Oliver H. Perry Papers, in Vertical File "P"; *George Tod Papers; *Allen Trimble Papers; *Elijah Wadsworth Family Papers; *Papers of John and Ashbel W. Walworth; *War of 1812: Collection of Papers, 1810–1820 (ca. 1 foot); *Elisha Whittlesey Papers and Addition; *James Winchester Papers (copies)

Columbus:

Ohio Historical Society:
*Quintus F. Atkins Papers; Ethan Allen Brown Papers on deposit from the Ohio State Library, Columbus; *John Cassil Papers; *Henry Clay Papers (copies); Moses Deming Papers; *James Denny Papers; *John Fuller Papers; *William Henry Harrison Papers; *Samuel Huntington Papers, also papers on deposit from the Ohio State Library, Columbus; *John Johnston Papers; *Joseph Kerr Papers; *James Kilbourn Papers; *Larwill Family Papers; *Duncan McArthur Papers; *Jared Mansfield Papers; *Marietta College Collection (microfilm); *Return J. Meigs, Jr., Papers, also papers on deposit from the Ohio State Library, Columbus; *Miscellaneous Military Documents Collections; *Nathan Newson Diary; *Perry's Victory and International Peace Centennial Commission; *John Robinson Diary; Edward Tiffin Papers; *Allen Trimble Papers; *William A. Trimble Papers; Joseph Vance Papers; Zalmon Wildman Papers; *Thomas Worthington Papers, also papers on deposit from the Ohio State Library, Columbus

Dayton:

Dayton-Montgomery County Public Library:
*Henry Brown-Robert Patterson Collection; *Patterson Family Papers

Fremont:

Rutherford B. Hayes Library:
*George Croghan Collection; *Sandusky River Region Records (transcripts from the U.S. National Archives and the British Public Record Office)

Oberlin:

Oberlin College Library:
*Orrin W. June Collection on the War of 1812 (102 items)

Springfield:

Clark County Historical Society:
*Samuel Black Journal; Dr. Isaac Kay Collection

Toledo:

Toledo-Lucas County Public Library:
*Capt. Daniel L. Cushing Diary, 1812–1813, and Orderly Book 1813–1814 (2 vols.); *one WHH letter; *War of 1812 Papers, 1810–1815 (7 items)

Oregon

Eugene:

University of Oregon Library:
*McKean-Smith Collection of Presidential Autographs

Pennsylvania

Carlisle:

Dickinson College Library:
*one WHH letter
U.S. Army Military History Institute:
Amasiah Ford Papers

Erie:

Erie County Historical Society:
*John Kelso Papers; *James Scott Orderly Book; *Adamson Tannehill Orderly Book

Haverford:

Haverford College Library:
*The Quaker Collection

Philadelphia:

Historical Society of Pennsylvania:
*Connoroe Collection; *Ferdinand J. Dreer Collection; *Etting Collection; *Simon Gratz Collection (many subseries); *George Harrison Official Records; *Uselma Clarke Smith Collection of William Jones Papers; James Madison Papers; Miscellaneous Collection; Miscellaneous Collections of Autographs; *Daniel Parker Papers; *Society Collection

Pittsburgh:

Darlington Memorial Library, University of Pittsburgh:
*Diary of Charles Pentland, September 10, 1812–September 10, 1813; James Wilkinson Papers
Historical Society of Western Pennsylvania:
*Ebenezer Denny Account Books; *Greenbury Keen Journal; *Stanton Sholes Diary

Rhode Island

Newport:

Newport Historical Society:
*Oliver H. Perry and the Battle of Lake Erie, 1813 (clippings and scrapbooks); *William V. Taylor Account of the Battle of Lake Erie; **U.S.S. Lawrence* Logbook

Providence:

John Hay Library, Brown University:
Usher Parsons Family Papers

Tennessee

Chattanooga:

Chattanooga Public Library:
*John Gibbons Papers

Nashville:

Tennessee State Library and Archives:
Edmund Pendleton Gaines Papers; *James Winchester Papers, also papers on deposit from the Tennessee Historical Society
Vanderbilt University Library:
*James G. Stahlman Historical Collection

Texas

Austin:

E. C. Barker Texas History Center, University of Texas Library
*Anthony Butler Papers

Virginia

Charlottesville:

Alderman Library, University of Virginia:
*Joel Leftwich Papers; James Madison Papers

Richmond:

Virginia State Library:
*War of 1812 Records (26 vols. and 1,360 items)

Williamsburg:

Earl Gregg Swem Library, College of William and Mary:
David I. Bushnell Papers; *Francis Little Collection

West Virginia

Morgantown:

West Virginia University Library:
*James H. Carroll Papers

Wisconsin

Madison:

State Historical Society of Wisconsin:
Nicholas Boilvin Correspondence (1 box of photocopies from the U.S. National Archives); *Robert Dickson Papers; *Lyman C. Draper Manuscripts, including the following subseries: Daniel Boone Papers (C), Samuel Brady and Lewis Wetzel Papers (E), George Rogers Clark Papers (J), William Croghan Papers (N), Draper's Historical Miscellanies (Q), Draper's Notes (S), Thomas Forsyth Papers (T), Frontier Wars Papers (U), William Henry Harrison Papers (X), Simon Kenton Papers (BB), Kentucky Papers (CC), King's Mountain Papers (DD), Thomas Sumter Papers (VV), John Cleves Symmes Papers (WW), and Tecumseh Papers (YY); George Gibbs Papers; *Perry's Victory Centennial Comission Records; Records from the National Archives of Canada (transcripts, photocopies, and microfilm); *Eleazer D. Wood Papers

Notes

Introduction

1. Official Correspondence from Procter, National Archives of Canada, Record Group 8, British Military Record, Military "C" series.

The Battle of Lake Erie

1. Editor's note: In his article "A Failure of Command, Control, and Communication," Michael Palmer draws a different conclusion. According to Palmer, Elliott held his position in the American line rather than close with the *Queen Charlotte,* the vessel with which he was supposed to fight, because Perry gave no direct order to Elliott to pass the *Caledonia* and come forward. *Journal of Erie Studies* 17 (Fall 1988): 7–26. Altoff disagrees with Palmer's interpretation. See Gerald T. Altoff, "The Perry-Elliott Controversy," *Northwest Ohio Quarterly* 60 (Autumn 1988): 135–52.

2. The following sources were consulted in writing this paper:

Unpublished Primary Sources: Records of the Department of the Navy (Letters to Officers, Ships of War; Officers Letters; Masters Commandant Letters; Captains Letters; Private Letters), Record Group 45, National Archives, Washington, D.C.; Letterbooks of Commodore Isaac Chauncey, Letterbook of Oliver Hazard Perry (March 1813–June 1813), Oliver Hazard Perry Papers (1795–1864), William Clements Library, University of Michigan, Ann Arbor, Michigan.

Published Primary Sources: Anthony Wayne Parkway Board, *Document Transcriptions of the War of 1812 in the Northwest,* 10 vols. (Columbus: The Ohio Historical Society, 1962); Daniel Dobbins, *The Dobbins Papers,* vol. 8, ed. Frank H. Severance (Buffalo: Publications of the Buffalo Historical Society, 1905); Jesse D. Elliott, *Speech of Com. Jesse Duncan Elliott, U.S.N. Delivered in Hagerstown, MD, on November 14, 1843* (Philadelphia: G. B. Zieber & Company, 1844); Usher Parsons, *Battle of Lake Erie, A Discourse Delivered Before the Rhode Island Historical Society on February 16, 1853* (Palmyra, N.Y.: Benjamin T. Albro, Printer, 1854); *Prologue to Victory, General Orders, Fort Meigs to Put-in-Bay, April–September, 1813,* in *Kentucky Historical Society Register* 60 (1963); United States Congress, "Samuel Hambleton's Account of the Distribution of Prize Money on Lake Erie," and

"List of Killed and Wounded on Board of the United States' squadron, under Command of O. H. Perry, Esq., in the Battle of September 10, 1813," *American State Papers: Naval Affairs,* vol. 1 (Washington: Gales & Seaton, 1832).

Published Secondary Sources: Pierre Berton, *Flames Across the Border* (Boston: Little, Brown and Company, 1981); Harrison Bird, *War for the West 1790–1813* (New York: Oxford University Press, 1971); David C. Bunnell, *Travels and Adventures of David C. Bunnell During Twenty-Three Years of a Seafaring Life* (Palmyra, N.Y.: J. H. Bortles, Printer, 1831); Hon. Tristam Burges, *Battle of Lake Erie* (Providence, R.I.: Brown & Cady, 1839); Howard Chappelle, *The History of the American Sailing Navy* (New York: W. W. Norton & Co., 1949); Howard Chappelle, *The History of American Sailing Ships* (New York: W. W. Norton & Co., 1955); "Citizen of New York," *A Biographical Notice of Com. Jesse D. Elliott Containing a Review of the Controversy Between Him and the Late Commodore Perry* (Philadelphia: For the Author, 1835); James Fenimore Cooper, *History of the Navy of the United States of America,* 2 vols. (Philadelphia: Lea and Blanchard, 1840); Richard Dillon, *We Have Met the Enemy* (New York: McGraw-Hill, 1978); Captain W. W. Dobbins, *History of the Battle of Lake Erie and Reminiscences of the Flagships "Lawrence" and "Niagara"* (Erie: Ashby Printing Co., 1913); Robert J. Dodge, *The Battle of Lake Erie* (Fostoria, Ohio: Gray Printing Co., 1967); Charles J. Dutton, *Oliver Hazard Perry* (New York: Longmans, Green and Co., 1935); Alex R. Gilpin, *The War of 1812 in the Old Northwest* (East Lansing: Michigan State University, 1958); Benson J. Lossing, *The Pictorial Field-Book of the War of 1812* (New York: Harper and Brothers, 1869); Olin L. Lyman, *Commodore Oliver Hazard Perry and the War on the Lakes* (New York: New Amsterdam Book Co., 1905); Alex. Slidell Mackenzie, *Commodore Perry, His Life and Achievements,* centennial edition (Akron: J. K. Richardson & Sons, 1910); Alfred Thayer Mahan, *Sea Power in Its Relation to the War of 1812,* 2 vols. (New York: Little, Brown and Company, 1903; reprint, New York: Greenwood Press, 1968); James Cooke Mills, *Oliver Hazard Perry and the Battle of Lake Erie* (Detroit: John Phelps, 1913); Newport Historical Society, *Items of Interest Concerning Oliver Hazard Perry and the War of 1812 in Newport* (Newport, R.I.: Mercury Publishing Co., 1913); John N. Niles, *The Life of Oliver Hazard Perry* (Hartford: William S. Marsh, 1820); Usher Parsons, *Brief Sketches of the Officers Who Were in the Battle of Lake Erie* (Albany, N.Y.: J. Munsell, 1862); Theodore Roosevelt, *The Naval War of 1812* (New York and London: G. P. Putnam's Sons, 1882); Max Rosenberg, *The Building of Perry's Fleet on Lake Erie, 1812–1813* (Harrisburg: Pennsylvania Historical and Museum Commission, 1968); Glenn Tucker, *Poltroons and Patriots,* 2 vols. (New York: Bobbs-Merrill Co., 1954); Glenn Tucker, *Dawn Like Thunder, the Barbary Wars and the Birth of the U.S. Navy* (New York: The Bobbs-Merrill Co., 1963).

Unpublished Secondary Sources: Gerard T. Altoff, "Deep Water Sailors—Shallow Water Soldiers" (unpublished manuscript, Perry's Victory & International Peace Monument, Put-in-Bay, Ohio, January 1988).

Artillery and its Influence on Naval Tactics

Michael Lewis, "Armada Guns: A Comparative Study of English and Spanish Armaments," section 1, "Classification," *Mariner's Mirror* 28 (January 1942): 44.

1. Frederick C. Drake, "Command Decisions and Combined Operations: Commodore James Lucas Yeo," paper presented at the Joint Meeting of the North American Society for Oceanic History and the Canadian Nautical Research Society, Kingston, Ontario, May 22, 1987; and "Commodore Sir James Lucas Yeo and Governor General

Sir George Prevost: A Study in Command Relations, 1813–1814," paper presented at the 8th Naval History Symposium, September 24–26, 1987, Annapolis, Maryland (the latter to be published in conference proceedings).

2. The best source is Chauncey's Letterbooks, William Clements Library, University of Michigan, Ann Arbor; Chauncey to the Secretary of the Navy, 26 September 1812, Chauncey Letterbooks, also in Captain's Letters, and quoted in Alfred T. Mahan, *Sea Power in Its Relations to the War of 1812,* 2 vols. (Boston: Little, Brown and Company, 1905), 1:361–62; Charles P. Stacey, "Another Look at the Battle of Lake Erie," *Canadian Historical Review* 39 (1958): 45–46; E. A. Cruikshank, "The Contest for the Command of Lake Ontario in 1812 and 1813," *Transactions of the Royal Society of Canada,* section 2, 3d ser., 10 (September 1916): 165.

3. See JKL, "Sir James Lucas Yeo," *Dictionary of National Biography* 21 (Oxford, England: Oxford University Press, 1917); John C. Spurr, "The Royal Navy's Presence in Kingston, Part I: 1813–1836," *Historic Kingston* 25 (March 1977): 63–64; John C. Spurr, "James Lucas Yeo," *Dictionary of Canadian Biography* (Toronto: University of Toronto Press, 1987), 5:874–77; William James, *Naval History of Great Britain from 1793–1820* (London, England: R. Bentley, 1837), 5:73–77; Court Martial of Sir James Lucas Yeo for the loss of *HMS Southampton,* 13 February 1813, Public Records Office, London, England, Admiralty Court Martial Records, Adm 1/5434.

4. Michael Lewis, "Armada Guns: A Comparative Study of English and Spanish Armaments," section 1, "Classification"; section 2, "The Guns of the Queen's Ships, 1569–99"; section 3, "The Queen's Ships in July, 1588," section 4, "The Auxiliary English Fleet," *Mariner's Mirror* 28 (January–October 1942): 41–73, 104–47, 231–45, 259–90. The quotation is from section 1:41–42.

5. An example is given by James, *Naval History,* 1:401, note W:

The *Magnamine*		The *Prudente*
26 long 24s	Main Deck	26 long 12s
12 long 12s	Quarter Deck &	12 long 6s
6 carronades 6s	Forecastle	6 carronades
44		44

The *Magnamine* thus threw total metal of 804 lbs.; the *Prudente,* 492 lbs.

6. "The Return of Vessels, Arms, and Men" for Chauncey's squadron, National Archives, Washington, D.C., Record Group 45; "Statement of the Number and Force of His Majesty's Squadron upon Lake Ontario," Yeo at the Head of the Lake Ontario to Warren, Halifax, 29 September 1813, National Archives of Canada, Adm 1/504, p. 324. Slightly different figures are given in E. A. Cruikshank, "The Contest for the Command of Lake Ontario in 1812 and 1813," 188.

In reality, Yeo's squadron was inferior to Chauncey's by only 82 pounds in total weight of metal, by 292 men in squadron numbers, and by almost 1,000 tons because his vessels were very much smaller. Yeo's broadside was mainly a heavy carronade broadside. He had only nineteen long guns in his squadron throwing total shot of 330 pounds. Only eleven guns, including his pivot guns, could fire in any one broadside, with 201 pounds. Yeo's seventy-two carronades, however, fired 2,312 pounds of total metal, and in any one broadside thirty-six could fire 1,156 pounds of shot. Chauncey's balance was much better. In summer 1813, he normally had sixty-four long guns in his squadron and they fired a total of 1,181 pounds of shot. In addition, his forty-eight carronades fired 1,248 pounds. Of the sixty-four long guns that Chauncey had, no less than forty-eight could be fired in any one broadside, discharging 815 pounds of metal, because of the preponderance of pivot guns. The carronades were usually fixed on slides or on carriages, and in a broadside twenty-four would fire 624 pounds of shot. Thus while any one broadside of Yeo's fired 1,357 pounds to Chauncey's 1,439, the latter had a 4 to 1 advantage in long guns broadside metal, while Yeo had a 2 to 1 advantage with carronade fire. Obviously, Yeo could only engage with a prospect of success at close range, when his heavy carronades would equalize his broadside disadvantage.

If broadside metal had been the only factor to consider, Chauncey could well have been more successful than he proved to be, for his own flagship *General Pike* equipped entirely with long guns, by its very size and ability to absorb punishment, could have gained the superiority on the lake on its own. Chauncey could fire on Yeo with long guns that could cripple his ships by disabling rigging, sails, and guns, and leave him unable to reply. One disabling factor for Chauncey was that before August 8, 1813, his schooners contained thirty-six of his sixty-four long guns, the remainder being in the *Pike*. Though Chauncey's first three war vessels, therefore, were within 4 pounds weight of broadside metal of Yeo's first three, their much greater size and range of long guns certainly made them more than a match for Yeo's squadron.

7. Michael Lewis, "Armada Guns," section 1: 44.

8. J. Fenimore Cooper, *The History of the Navy of the United States of America,* 2 vols. (New York: G. P. Putnam, 1854), 1:ix. Cooper justly pointed out the importance of the receiving power of a ship, that is the thickness of her scantling's ability to sustain injury and shelter her crew as of equal importance with weight of broadside alone:

> Every mode of rating is liable to some objection, and nothing is more fallacious than to estimate the power of a ship by the number of her guns. Two great elements of force enter into the composition of a vessel of war: the ability to annoy, and the ability to endure. A ship of one thousand tons burthen, armed with one heavy gun, might resist for a long time a dozen vessels of thirty tons, each armed with the same species of gun. This advantage would arise from the greater ability of the larger vessel to endure. On the other hand, the same ship, armed with one heavy gun, would probably capture a similar vessel armed with twenty light guns, her ability to annoy being the greatest.

9. Alfred T. Mahan, *Sea Power* 1:334, on the *Constitution—Guerriere* action wrote, "The customary, and upon the whole justest mode of estimating relative power, was by aggregate weight of shot discharged; and when, *as in this case,* the range is so close, that every gun comes into play, it is *perhaps* a useless refinement to insist on *qualifying* considerations" (my italics). Whether he was right as regards the particular frigate action he was discussing is open to debate but there Mahan showed not only the awareness of the qualifying considerations, but that they applied in most cases that were not outright broadside battles between forces equal in all-round strength, and very few actions in this war met this criterion.

10. As for example, C. S. Forester, *The Naval War of 1812* (London: M. Joseph, 1957), and F. F. Beirne, *The War of 1812* (New York: E. P. Dutton, 1949), both of whom give very general accounts of actions and few, if any, statistical details. Mahan himself shied away from broadside comparisons in many of the actions he described.

11. Frederick C. Drake, "A Loss of Mastery: The British Squadron on Lake Erie, May–September, 1813," *Journal of Erie Studies* 17 (Fall 1988): 47–75. On the shortage of transport craft, *see also* "Narrative of the Proceedings during the Command of Captain

Barclay of His Majesty's Squadron on Lake Erie," given in the Court Martial of Captain Barclay, 9 September 1814, Public Records Office, London, England, Adm 1/5445, pp. 34–35.

12. For the shifting size and the changing batteries of the Lake Erie vessels of the Canadian Provincial Marine, see A. H. Pye, Return of the Effective Strength of the Provincial Marine on the Rivers and Lakes in Canada, as per Returns last received, Quebec, 21 June 1811, PAC C 373, p. 23, in William Wood, *Select British Documents of the Canadian War of 1812,* Champlain Society Publications, nos. 13–15, 17, 4 vols. (Toronto: Champlain Society, 1920–28), 1:239; A. H. Pye, Proposed Establishment of the Provincial Marine Department for the Lakes and Rivers in Upper and Lower Canada, for the Year 1812, 30 August 1811, PAC C 728, p. 60, in Wood, *Select Documents* 1:246–47; A. H. Pye, Return of His Majesty's Provincial Marine on the Rivers and Lakes in the Upper and Lower Canada, 16 September 1811, PAC C 373, p. 28, in Wood, *Select Documents* 1:239–41; Report upon the Provincial Marine Establishment in Upper Canada, submitted for the consideration of His Excellency the Commander of the Forces, by Captn. Gray Actg. Deputy Qur. Mr. Genl., 24 February 1812, PAC C 728, p. 86, in Wood, *Select Documents* 1:254; Stacey, "Another Look at the Battle of Lake Erie," 43; F. Cleaver Bald, "The United States Shipyard on the River Rouge, Part II," *Inland Seas* 3 (1947): 71–72; C. Winton Clare, "A Shipbuilder's War," *Mariner's Mirror* 29 (July 1943): 142.

13. Barclay's naval arrangements, Naval Yard, Kingston, 5 May 1813, in Wood, *Select Documents* 2:113–15; Barclay at Kingston to Noah Freer at Quebec, Wolfe, Kingston, 9 May 1813, ibid., 2:115–18; Barclay's "Narrative," given in the Court Martial of Captain Barclay, 9 September 1814, Public Records Office, London, Adm 1/5445, p. 29.

14. Chauncey reported finding twenty-eight cannons at York, from 6- to 32-pounders, shot and munitions, "a great deal of which was put up in boxes and marked for Niagara and Malden." He reported to Secretary of the Navy William Jones that: "The store which the enemy burned was filled with cables, cordage, canvas, tools, and stores of every kind for the use of this Lake and Lake Erie, supposed to be worth $50,000. The loss of stores at this place will be an irreparable one to the enemy, for independent of the difficulty of transportation, the articles cannot be replaced in this country." Chauncey to the Secretary of the Navy, 7 May 1813, Chauncey Letterbooks; also quoted by Stacey, "Another Look at the Battle of Lake Erie," 45.

15. Testimony of Provincial Lieutenant Francis Purvis of the *Detroit,* and Lieutenant Stokoe of the *Queen Charlotte,* to the court, Barclay's Court Martial, 9 September 1814, Public Records Office, London, Adm 1/5445, pp. 22, 24–25. On Perry's squadron being built, see M. Rosenberg, *The Building of Perry's Fleet on Lake Erie, 1812–1813* (Harrisburg: Pennsylvania Historical and Museum Commission, 1968), passim, and on the guns see pp. 41–43. On Perry's careful reflections upon "naval Gunnery," see the Oliver H. Perry Letterbook, pp. 10–30; on his bringing the Black Rock guns, see Perry Letterbook, pp. 123 and 126. On the substitution of carronades for his long guns, see Oliver H. Perry to Christopher R. Perry, 9 August 1813, and the "Statement of the force of the United States squadron," Perry Papers, William Clements Library, University of Michigan, Ann Arbor.

16. Barclay to Prevost, 16 July 1813, and with the same letter dated Long Point, 16 July 1813, in Wood, *Select Documents* 2:250, 257–59.

17. Prevost to Warren, Kingston, 24 June 1813, Public Records Office, London, Adm 1/503, p. 142.

18. A statement of the Force of His Majesty's Squadron employed on Lake Erie, Public Records Office, London, Adm 1/2737, p. 5; also in Wood, *Select Documents* 2:251–52.

19. Procter to Prevost, 29 August 1813, Barclay to Yeo, 1 September 1813, in Wood, *Select Documents* 2:226, 267–69.

20. Procter to Prevost, 19 and 26 August 1813, in Wood, *Select Documents* 2:263, 265.

21. Barclay to Yeo, 6 September 1813, in Wood, *Select Documents* 2:293; Procter to Freer, 6 September 1813, ibid., 2:269–70; Narrative to the Court Martial, 9 September 1814, Public Records Office, London, Adm 1/5445, p. 41.

22. Statement of the force of the United States squadron September 10, Perry to the Secretary of the Navy, 13 September 1813, *American State Papers Naval Affairs,* 1:294–97; compare with, "A statement of the Forces of the American Squadron, as last reconnoitered in the Harbor of Presque Isle, June 28, 1813," Public Records Office, Adm 1/2737, p. 5.

23. Mahan, *Sea Power* 2:77.

24. Roosevelt, *Naval War of 1812,* 215.

25. James, *Naval History* 6:249.

26. Barclay, "Narrative," and Barclay to Yeo, 12 September 1813, Adm 1/5445, p. 53; Adm 1/505, p. 191, in Wood, *Select Documents* 2:275.

27. That would give 84 pounds plus the long 18 as the broadside of the other side of the ship, totaling 102 pounds.

28. Mahan, *Sea Power 1812* 2:91.

29. Perry's statement of the British force, *American State Papers Naval Affairs* 1:294; *Niles Weekly Register* 5:62.

30. This shows that the pivot guns were Perry's tactical edge against an ill-fought action. There is a similar conclusion about Perry's guns in an article critical of him, by Michael A. Palmer, "A Failure of Command, Control, and Communications," *Journal of Erie Studies* 17 (Fall 1988): 7–26, esp. 24 and n. 37 (which give slightly different figures).

The Honor of the Flag Had Not Suffered

1. Frank H. Severence, ed., "The Dobbins Papers," in *Publications of the Buffalo Historical Society,* vol. 8 (Buffalo: Buffalo Historical Society, 1905); W. W. Dobbins, *History of the Battle of Lake Erie,* 2d ed. (Erie, Penn.: Ashby Printing Company, 1913).

2. Howard Chapelle, *The History of the American Sailing Navy* (New York: W. W. Norton and Co., 1949).

3. A. T. Mahan, *Sea Power in its Relation to the War of 1812,* 2 vols. (Boston: Little, Brown and Company, 1905), 2:94–95.

4. Theodore Roosevelt, *The Naval War of 1812,* 2 vols. (New York: Collier, 1882; review of review edition, New York: G. P. Putnam's Sons, 1910), 2:331.

5. Ibid., 330.

6. James Barnes, *Naval Actions of the War of 1812* (New York: Harper & Brothers, 1896), 139–56.

7. Alexander Clark Casselman, *Richardson's War of 1812; With Notes and a Life of the Author* (Toronto: Historical Publishing Co., 1902), 215–18.

8. John Marshall, *Royal Naval Biography* (London: printed for Longman, Hurst, Rees, Orme and Brown, 1831), vol. 3, pt. 1:194.

9. Ibid.

10. Yeo to Secretary of the Admiralty, 10 October 1813, National Archives of Canada (hereafter NAC), Captains letters, Adm 1/2736, microfilm reel B-2941.

11. Ibid.

12. William F. Coffin, *1812: The War and Its Moral: A Canadian Chronicle* (Montreal: J. Lovell, 1864), 218–19.

13. Mahan, *Sea Power* 2:95; E. A. Cruikshank, "The Contest for Command of Lake Erie in 1812–1813," in *The Defended Border: Upper Canada and the War of 1812*, ed. Moris Zaslow and Wesley B. Turner (Toronto: Macmillan Publishing Co., 1964), 84–104; James Cooke Mills, *Oliver Hazard Perry and the Battle of Lake Erie* (Detroit: J. Phelps, 1913), 89–90; Dobbins, *Battle of Lake Erie*, 47–51. William Kingsford, *The History of Canada*, vol. 8 (Toronto: Rosewell and Hutchinson, 1895), does not even mention the building and escape of Perry's fleet.

14. Dobbins, *Battle of Lake Erie*, 47–51.

15. Egerton Ryerson, *The Loyalists of America and Their Times*, 2 vols. (Toronto: W. Briggs, 1880), 2:254–55.

16. Benjamin Lossing, *The Pictorial Field Book of the War of 1812* (New York: Harper and Brothers, 1869), 515n.

17. Ibid.

18. C. H. J. Snider, *In the Wake of the EighteenTwelvers; Fights and Flights of Frigates and Fore-'n-'Afters in the War of 1812–1815 on the Great Lakes* (London: John Lane, 1913).

19. But see Robert Buckie, " 'His Majesty's Flag Has Not Been Tarnished': The Role of Robert Heriot Barclay," *The Journal of Erie Studies* 17 (Fall 1988): 85–102. Buckie establishes that Barclay's school teacher in Kettle, Scotland, had been John Strachan. It was through Strachan's efforts that the merchants of Quebec and London honored Barclay with testimonial dinners and gifts of plate. See Letter to Colonel Harvey, in *The John Strachan Letter Book: 1812–1813*, ed. George W. Spragge (Toronto: Ontario Historical Society, 1946), 85.

20. Barclay's narrative, court martial proceedings, Adm 1/5445, printed in William Wood, *Selective British Documents of the Canadian War of 1812*, 4 vols. (Toronto: The Champlain Society, 1923), 2:298.

21. R. H. Mackenzie, *The Trafalgar Roll* (London: Allen, 1913), 220, 224–25; Marshall, *Royal Naval Biography*; National Maritime Museum, Greenwich, *The Commissioned Sea Officers of the Royal Navy 1660–1815* (personal annotated copy, Commander C. G. Pitcairn-Jones, [1954]), 1:40.

22. Mahan, *Sea Power* 2:80ff. concludes that Barclay had victory in his grasp "changed to defeat by the use Perry made of the vessel preserved to him intact by the over-caution of his second [Jesse Elliott]."

23. Howard H. Peckham, "Commodore Perry's Captive," *Ohio History* 72 (July 1963): 220–27.

24. Barclay to Sir John J. Douglas, 13 February 1822, War of 1812 Papers, vol. 4, William L. Clements Library, University of Michigan, Ann Arbor.

25. NAC, Adm12/168, vol. 721, 1815 and 1831.

26. Obituary dated 19 March 1831, Quebec *Mercury*. I am indebted to Hugh Halliday of the Canadian War Museum for this reference.

27. Philéas Gagnon, "Frédéric Rolette," *Bulletin de Récherche Historique* 1 (1895): 20–27; P. G. Roy, *Toutes Petites Choses Du Régime Anglais* (Quebec: Editions Garneau, 1946), 1e. series: 257; NAC, Record Group 1, L3L, Lower Canada Land Petitions, vol. 74, Microfilm reel C–2522 and vol. 169, Microfilm reel C–25598; Record Group 8,

"C" series, vol. 207, 30–33, vol. 677, 127–31, vol. 688B, 137–43, vol. 691–92, 695, 728, 730, 732–34, passim, vol. 738, 162.

28. Notes by Mrs. Stephen Heward preserved by S. A. Heward, 6 December 1949, referring among other paintings to that of the Battle of Lake Erie showing the *Detroit* dismasted and *Queen Charlotte* badly knocked about, and the American ship *Niagara* and another with their colors flying.

29. See W. A. B. Douglas, "The Anatomy of Naval Incompetence: The Provincial Marine in Defence of Upper Canada Before 1813," *Ontario History* 1 (September 1979): 3–26.

30. William Bell Papers, National Archives, Ottawa, Manuscript Group 24 F3/1; C. P. Stacey, "Another Look at the Battle of Lake Erie," in *The Defended Border,* 105–13; Douglas, "The Anatomy of Naval Incompetence."

31. Bell's memorial of 10 June 1818, and enclosures; Bell to William Hamilton, 24 June 1818, thanking him for the letter which resulted in the Treasury Board giving him the allowance which Navy Board regulations permitted for Dockyard Officers. There is also a letter in the Bell Papers from the Treasury Board explaining the compensation and allowances he will receive. It appears to be wrongly dated 2 July 1816, at which time he was still in his position at Kingston dockyard. Other evidence suggests it should be dated 2 July 1818. Subsequent correspondence in this collection provides a record of his success as a shipbuilder after the War of 1812. NAC Manuscript Group 24 F3/1.

32. C. P. Stacey, "The War of 1812 in Canadian History," in *The Defended Border,* 337.

The Battle of Lake Erie and its Consequences

1. Details of the British actions immediately after the Battle of Lake Erie can be found in the extensive testimony presented at H. Procter's court-martial. National Archives of Canada (hereafter NAC), WO71/243. A good summary of the testimony is contained in D. Sugden, *Tecumseh's Last Stand* (Oklahoma: University of Oklahoma Press, 1985).

2. H. Procter to Sir G. Prevost, 9 August 1813, *Collections of Michigan Pioneer and Historical Society* (Lansing: Thorp and Godfrey et al., 1874–1929), 15:347.

3. Ibid.

4. Procter to Prevost, 18, 19 August 1813, *Michigan Pioneer Collection* 15:354, 355.

5. Barclay to Yeo, 1 September 1813, NAC, Record Group 8I, 730:126–28.

6. Unaddressed to Procter, 22 August 1813, *Michigan Pioneer Collection* 15:357.

7. De Rottenburg to Colonel Baynes, 10 September 1813, *Michigan Pioneer Collection* 15:375.

8. Barclay's statement to the court martial investigating his conduct during the Battle of Lake Erie, NAC, Manuscript Group 12, Adm1/5445.

9. Ibid.

10. Testimony at court martial of Procter, NAC, WO71/243.

11. R. Allen, *The British Indian Department and the Frontier in North America, 1755–1830,* Canadian Historic Sites Occasional Papers, no. 14 (Ottawa: Queen's Printer, 1973).

12. Procter was subsequently found negligent in his conduct of the retreat and the disposition of his men to meet the American attack. NAC, WO71/243.

13. Proclamation by W. H. Harrison and O. Perry, 18 October 1813, Duncan McArthur Papers, United States Library of Congress, Washington, D.C.; "The Occupation of Michigan, an Incident in the History of Military Government," *Michigan Law Review* 22 (April 1924): 509–20.

14. Harrison to Armstrong, 23 February 1814, Letters Received by the Secretary of War, National Archives, Washington, D.C., Record Group 107, Microcopy 221, Reel 53.

15. D. Bridges, "In Defence of a Homeland: Indians at War Along the Detroit Frontier, 1790–1815" (unpublished paper, Environment Canada, Canadian Parks Service, Ontario Regional Office, Cornwall, Ontario, n.d.); A. Gilpin, *The War of 1812 in the Old Northwest* (Toronto: Ryerson Press, 1958), 227.

16. Cass to Puthuff, 23 October 1813, Lewis Cass Papers, Burton Historical Collection, Detroit Public Library, Detroit, Michigan.

17. Cass to Larwill, 6 December 1813, Cass Papers.

18. Report by Lieutenant Larwill on his capture and escape, Larwill Papers, Burton Historical Collection, Detroit Public Library, Detroit, Michigan; Lieutenant Medcalf's official report cited in M. Coleman, "The Action at McCrea's House" (unpublished paper, Environment Canada, Canadian Parks Service, Ontario Regional Office, Cornwall, Ontario, n.d.).

19. McCormick to Colonel Miller, 16 September 1814, McArthur Papers; W. R. Riddell, "The Ancaster 'Bloody Assize' of 1814," in *The Defended Border: Upper Canada and the War of 1812,* ed. M. Zaslow and W. B. Turner (Toronto: Macmillan Publishing Co., 1964).

20. J. M. Hitsman, *The Incredible War of 1812* (Toronto: University of Toronto Press, 1965), 177–79.

21. Monthly return for Detroit and Dependencies, January 1814, McArthur Papers.

22. Monthly return for Detroit and Dependencies, April 1814, McArthur Papers.

23. Armstrong to McArthur, 13 July 1814, McArthur Papers.

24. Croghan to Harrison, 15 May 1814, McArthur Papers.

25. Todd to Officer Commanding at Detroit, 20 July 1814; Court-martial of Captain Gray, 14 July 1814, McArthur Papers; Court-martial held at Major Graham's quarters on Private Hyatt Leasure for desertion, 24 August 1814, McArthur Papers.

26. Croghan to McArthur, 22 May 1814, McArthur Papers.

27. Harrison to Secretary of War, 23 January 1814, cited in P. Couture, "War and Society on the Detroit Frontier, 1791–1815" (unpublished paper, Environment Canada, Canadian Parks Service, Ontario Regional Office, Cornwall, Ontario, n.d.).

28. Croghan to McArthur, 22 May 1814, McArthur Papers.

29. McArthur to Armstrong, 8 June 1814, McArthur Papers.

30. McArthur to Croghan, 6 June 1814, McArthur Papers.

31. Miller to McArthur, 16 September 1814, McArthur Papers.

32. Cass to unaddressed, 16 September 1814, Cass Papers.

33. Gratoit to McArthur, 22 November 1814, McArthur Papers.

34. Proclamation by Colonel Miller, September 1814, McArthur Papers; J. Anderson, *A Short History of the Life of John Anderson,* cited in P. Couture, "War and Society on the Detroit Frontier."

35. Return of Claims for Western District, NAC, Record Group 19, E5A, vol. 3728.

36. Petition to McArthur, 12 October 1814, NAC, Manuscript Group 30, E66, 14/38.

37. Cass to Secretary of War, 4 September 1814, Cass Papers.

38. E. A. Cruikshank, "The County of Norfolk in the War of 1812," in *The Defended Border,* 237.

39. McArthur to Monroe, 6 February 1814, Butler to McArthur, 15 February 1815, both in McArthur Papers.

Tecumseh's Native Allies

1. Harrison to the Secretary of War, 15 July 1801, Hyacinth Lasselle Papers, Indiana State Library, Indianapolis.

2. Ibid.; William Burnett to Robert Innes and Co., 20 December 1798, in *Letter Book of William Burnett,* ed. Wilbur Cunningham (n.p.: Fort Miami Heritage Society of Michigan, 1967), 112; Burnett to George Gillespie, 30 May 1800, ibid., 129.

3. Grant Foreman, *The Last Trek of the Indians* (Chicago: University of Chicago Press, 1946), 17–32. For the specifics of these treaties, see Charles Kappler, ed., *Indian Treaties, 1778–1883,* 2 vols. (New York: Interland Publishing Co., 1972), passim.

4. Gerrard Hopkins, *A Mission to the Indians from the Committee of the Baltimore to Fort Wayne in 1804* (Philadelphia: T. Elwood Zell, 1862), 160–75; Paul Woehrmann, *At the Headwaters of the Maumee* (Indianapolis: Indiana Historical Society, 1971), 110–41.

5. William Wells to Henry Dearborn, 24 December 1808, National Archives, Washington, D.C., Records of the Office of the Secretary of War, Letters Received by the Secretary, Main Series, M221, Roll 33, 1257; Wells to Dearborn, 29 December 1808, ibid., 1272; Wells to Dearborn, 16 January 1809, ibid., 1317; Thomas Jefferson to the Potawatomi, December 1808, Potawatomi File, Great Lakes—Ohio Valley Indian Archives, Bloomington, Indiana. See also Hopkins, *A Mission to the Indians,* 186–91; and Woehrman, *At the Headwaters of the Maumee,* 189.

6. John Johnston to William Irvine, 9 August 1804, Johnston to Dearborn, 4 May 1805, Frank J. Jones Collection, Cincinnati Historical Society; Reginald Horsman, *Matthew Elliott, British Indian Agent* (Detroit: Wayne State University Press, 1964), 146.

7. Speech by Lord Dorchester, 10 February 1794, in *The Correspondence of Lieutenant Governor John Graves Simcoe,* ed. Ernest A. Cruikshank, 5 vols. (Toronto: Ontario Historical Society, 1923–1931), 2:149–50; Thomas Pasteur to Anthony Wayne, 8 March 1794, Potawatomi File, Great Lakes Indian Archives; Simcoe to Lord Dorchester, 29 April 1794, *Collections of the Michigan Pioneer and Historical Society,* 40 vols. (Lansing: Thorp and Godfrey, et al., 1874–1929), 24:659–60; Horsman, *Matthew Elliott,* 93–95.

8. Reginald Horsman, "The British Indian Department and the nce to General Anthony Wayne," *Mississippi Valley Historical Review* 44 (September 1962): 282; Speech by Tecumseh, 18 September 1813, in *Messages and Letters of William Henry Harrison,* ed. Logan Esarey, 2 vols. (Indianapolis: Indiana Historical Commission, 1922), 2:541–43.

9. James Henry Craig to William Thornton, 6 December 1807, British Colonial Office Records, Series 42, 136, 153–58; Francis Gore to Craig, 5 January 1808, ibid., p. 167. See also William Claus to Gore, 27 February 1808, William Claus Papers, National Archives of Canada (hereafter NAC), Manuscript Group 19, vol. 9, 177–81.

10. Harrison to the Secretary of War, 15 July 1801, in Esarey, *Harrison Letters,* 1:25–31; Harrison to the Indian Council, 12 August 1802, ibid., 52–54; Secretary of

War to Harrison, 23 February 1802, in *The Territorial Papers of the United States,* ed. Clarence E. Carter, 27 vols. (Washington: Government Printing Office, 1934–61), 7:48–50. See also George Ironside to Prideaux Selby, 23 December 1804, *Michigan Pioneer Collection,* 23:37; Speech by Little Turtle, December 1801, in Hopkins, *A Mission to the Indians,* 171; and John Heckewelder, *History, Manners, and Customs of the Indian Nations* (Philadelphia: Historical Society of Philadelphia, 1876), 220–23.

11. James Mooney, *The Ghost Dance Religion and the Sioux Outbreak of 1890,* Fourteenth Annual Report of the Bureau of American Ethnology, 2 pts. (Washington: Bureau of American Ethnology, 1896), 2:672–73; Benjamin Lossing, *Pictorial Field Book of the War of 1812* (New York: Harper and Brothers, 1869), 188–89; Vernon Kinietz and Erminie Wheeler-Voegelin, eds., *Shawnese Traditions: C. C. Trowbridge's Account, Occasional Contributions From the Museum of Anthropology of the University of Michigan,* No. 9 (Ann Arbor: University of Michigan Press, 1939), 41–42; Benjamin Drake, *Life of Tecumseh* (New York: Arno Press, 1969), 87.

12. Speech by Le Maigouis, 4 May 1807, Letters Received by the Secretary of War, Unregistered Series, National Archives, Washington, D.C., M222, Roll 2, 859–61; Thomas Forsyth to William Clark, 15 January 1827, Thomas Forsyth Papers, Draper Manuscripts, 9T51–54, State Historical Society of Wisconsin, Madison; Noel E. Schutz, Jr., "The Study of Shawnee Myth in an Ethnographic and Ethnohistorical Perspective" (Ph.D. diss., Indiana University, 1975), 178–79, 235. See also Harry Emilius Stocker, *A History of the Moravian Mission Among the Indians on the White River in Indiana* (Bethlehem, Penn.: Times Publishing Co., 1917), 106.

13. Harrison to the Delawares, 1806, in Esarey, *Harrison Letters,* 1:182–84; "On the Prophet," George Winter Papers, Tippecanoe County Historical Society, Lafayette, Indiana; Entry for 18 April 1806, Diary of the Little Indian Congregation on the White River for the Year 1806, in *The Moravian Mission on White River: Diaries and Letters, May 5, 1779, to November 12, 1806, Indiana Historical Collections,* ed. Lawrence Henry Gipson (Indianapolis: Indiana Historical Bureau, 1938), 23:421–22.

14. "On the Prophet," Winter Papers, Tippecanoe County Historical Society; Mooney, *The Ghost Dance Religion* 2:674; Drake, *Life of Tecumseh,* 91; Entry for 16 June 1806, in Joseph Badger, *A Memoir of Joseph Badger* (Hudson, Ohio: Sawyer, Ingersoll and Co., 1851), 147.

15. William Wells to the Secretary of War, 19 April 1807, Ottawa File, Great Lakes Indian Archives; Wells to the Secretary of War, 25 April 1807, ibid.

16. Thomas Worthington and Duncan McArthur to Thomas Kirker, 3 September 1807, Simon Kenton Papers, Draper Manuscripts, 7BB48; Drake, *Life of Tecumseh,* 96–97; Entries for 10 June–15 July 1808, Diary of William Claus, Claus Papers, NAC, Manuscript Group 19, 9, 206–15; Francis Gore to James Craig, 27 July 1808, ibid., Record Group 10, vol. 3; Harrison to the Secretary of War, 6 August 1810, in Esarey, *Harrison Letters* 11:456–59.

17. See Glenn Tucker, *Tecumseh: Vision of Glory* (New York: Russell and Russell, 1973), and Alvin M. Josephy, Jr., *The Patroit Chiefs: A Chronicle of American Indian Leadership* (New York: The Viking Press, 1961).

18. Ruth Landes, *The Prairie Potawatomi: Tradition and Ritual in the Twentieth Century* (Madison: University of Wisconsin Press, 1970), 51–52, 89; Statement by Thomas Forsyth, Tecumseh Papers, Draper Manuscripts, 8YY57; Draper's Notes, Draper Manuscripts, 26S90; Wells to Dearborn, 7 January 1808, Potawatomi File, Great Lakes Indian Archives; Wells to the Secretary of War, 20 April 1808, in Carter, *Territorial Papers* 7:555–60.

19. Richard McAfee, *History of the Late War in the Western Country* (Lexington: Worsley and Smith, 1816), 298; Wells to Dearborn, 24 December 1808, Records of the Office of the Secretary of War, Letters Received by the Secretary, Main Series, M221, Roll 33, 1257; Thomas Jefferson to the Potawatomi, December 1808, Potawatomi File, Great Lakes Indian Archives; Hopkins, *A Mission to the Indians,* 186–89.

20. Wells to Dearborn, 29 December 1808, Records of the Office of the Secretary of War, M221, Roll 33, 1272; Wells to Dearborn, 16 January 1809, ibid., 1317; Hopkins, *A Mission to the Indians,* 190–91; John Lalime to William Clark, 26 May 1811, in Esarey, *Harrison Letters* 1:511; Clark to Eustis, 24 May 1811, Potawatomi File, Great Lakes Indian Archives; Samuel Levering to Ninian Edwards, 12 August 1811, in Carter, *Territorial Papers* 26:175–79.

21. Matthew Elliott to William Claus, 14 July 1812, Wyandot File, Great Lakes Indian Archives; Elliott to Claus, 26 July 1812, NAC, Record Group 10, vol. 28, 16394–95; Milo M. Quaife, *War on the Detroit: The Chronicles of Thomas Vercheres de Boucherville and the Capitulation by an Ohio Volunteer* (Chicago: The Lakeside Press, 1940), 81–84, 256–59; William F. Coffin, *1812: The War and its Moral: A Canadian Chronicle* (Montreal: John Lovell, 1864), 199–200.

22. Forsyth to Benjamin Howard, 7 September 1812, in Carter, *Territorial Papers* 26:261–65; R. David Edmunds, *The Potawatomis: Keepers of the Fire* (Norman: University of Oklahoma Press, 1978), 186–88; Hull to Eustis, 26 August 1812, *Michigan Pioneer Collection* 40:460–69; Unknown to the Secretary of War, 8 September 1812, Records of the Office of the Secretary of War, M221, Roll 6, 2568–69; Muir to Procter in *Richardson's War of 1812,* ed. Alexander C. Casselman (Toronto: Coles Publishing Company, 1974), 296–300.

23. Procter to Roger Shaeffe, 13 January 1813, *Michigan Pioneer Collection* 15:215–16; Peter Chambers to Noah Freer, 24 April–5 May 1813, ibid., 15:289–91; Forsyth to Clark, 20 July 1813, Potawatomi File, Great Lakes Indian Archives; McAfee, *History of the Late War,* 264–77.

24. Duncan McArthur to the Secretary of War, 6 October 1813, *Michigan Pioneer Collection* 40:535–36; D. Cameron to Matthew Elliott, 25 March 1814, ibid., 15:524; "Report from the Indian Department," Spring 1814, ibid., 15:553; Thomas Posey to the Secretary of War, 12 November 1814, in Esarey, *Harrison Letters* 2:665; Statement by Thomas Forsyth, Tecumseh Papers, Draper Manuscripts, 8YY57. The most complete biographical sketch of Main Poc can be found in R. David Edmunds, "Main Poc: Potawatomi Wabeno," *American Indian Quarterly* 9 (Summer 1985): 259–72.

25. Thomas Worthington and Duncan McArthur to Thomas Kirker, 22 September 1807, Simon Kenton Papers, Draper Manuscripts, 7BB48; R. David Edmunds, *The Shawnee Prophet* (Lincoln: University of Nebraska Press, 1983), 61; Casselman, *Richardson's War of 1812,* 296–99; Horsman, *Matthew Elliott,* 201–4. See also R. David Edmunds, *Tecumseh and the Quest for Indian Leadership* (Boston: Little, Brown and Company, 1985), 180.

26. Edmunds, *Tecumseh,* 182–84; Alec Gilpin, *The War of 1812 in the Old Northwest* (East Lansing: Michigan State University Press, 1958), 167.

27. John Sugden, *Tecumseh's Last Stand* (Norman: University of Oklahoma Press, 1985), 18, 35–36; Frederick W. Hodge, ed., *Handbook of American Indians North of Mexico,* 2 vols. (New York: Rowman and Littlefield, 1971), 2:235.

28. Sugden, *Tecumseh's Last Stand,* 203, 236; Edmunds, *Tecumseh,* 182; Casselman, *Richardson's War of 1812,* 71; Edmunds, *Shawnee Prophet,* 148.

29. Edmunds, *Tecumseh,* 169–73.

30. Sugden, *Tecumseh's Last Stand,* 36, 38, 88, 240; Horsman, *Matthew Elliott,* 228.

31. Report by Antoine LeClaire, 14 July 1812, in Carter, *Territorial Papers* 16:248–50; Edmunds, *The Potawatomis,* 185–87, 206, 220; Nehemiah Matson, *Memories of Shaubena* (Chicago: D. B. Cooke and Company, 1878), 26–29; Draper's Notes, Draper Manuscripts, 26S70; "Niscanauma's Talk to Whistler," 22 May 1815, Potawatomi File, Great Lakes Indian Archives.

32. Woehrmann, *At the Headwaters of the Maumee,* 189; Hopkins, *A Mission to the Indians,* 186–91; Edmunds, "Main Poc," 263–64; Edmunds, *The Potawatomis,* 185–87.

33. Two articles which focus upon Caldwell's career are Thomas G. Conway, "An Indian Politician and Entrepreneur in the Old Northwest," *The Old Northwest* 1 (Summer 1975); 51–62; and James Clifton, "Merchant, Soldier, Broker, Chief: A Corrected Obituary of Captain Billy Caldwell," *Journal of the Illinois State Historical Society* 71 (August 1978): 185–210. See also Edmunds, *The Potawatomis,* 172–275, passim.

34. Sugden, *Tecumseh's Last Stand,* 85–86, 196–200, 211–12.

35. James Dowd, *Built Like a Bear* (Fairfield, Wash.: Galleon Press, 1979).

36. Donald Jackson, ed., *Black Hawk: An Autobiography* (Urbanna: University of Illinois Press, 1964), 64; R. David Edmunds, "Black Hawk," *Timeline* 5 (April–May 1988): 23–27.

37. Ninian Edwards, *History of Illinois From 1778 to 1833* (Springfield: Illinois State Journal, 1870), 37–38; Depositions by James Moredaugh and Stephen Cole, August–September 1810, Ninian Edwards Papers, Chicago Historical Society; Edmunds, *The Potawatomis,* 189–91; Wallace Brice, *History of Fort Wayne* (Fort Wayne, Ind.: D. W. Jones and Son, 1868), 236–37.

38. A. M. Gibson: *The Kickapoos: Lords of the Middle Border* (Norman: University of Oklahoma Press, 1963), 67–68; Zachary Taylor to Harrison, 10 September 1812, in Esarey, *Harrison Letters,* 2:124–28; Hiram Beckwith, *The Illinois and Indiana Indians* (Chicago: Fergus Printing Co., 1884), 134–35.

39. Paul Radin, *The Winnebago Tribe* (Lincoln: University of Nebraska Press, 1970), 21–22; Statement by Joseph Barron, Winter Papers, Tippecanoe County Historical Society; Statement by Isaac Naylor, Eyewitness Account File, Tippecanoe Battleground Museum, Battleground, Indiana; Louise Phelps Kellogg, *The British Regime in Wisconsin and the Old Northwest* (New York: Da Capo Press, 1971), 317–18.

40. Edmunds, *Shawnee Prophet,* 184–90; R. David Edmunds, "The Thin Red Line: Tecumseh, the Prophet, and Shawnee Resistance," *Timeline* 4 (December 1987–January 1988): 2–19; Edmunds, *Tecumseh,* 213–25.

The Quest for Peace in the War of 1812

1. Lieutenant General Sir George Prevost, the captain-general and governor-in-chief of Canada, tried to arrange an armistice with Major General Henry Dearborn on the New York front in August 1812. Dearborn said that he did not have the authority to declare an armistice and referred the matter to Washington where it was disapproved. On September 30, 1813, Admiral Sir John Borlase Warren, the commander of the North American and West Indian Station, wrote to Secretary of State James Monroe proposing the cessation of warfare. Monroe replied on October 24 that the abandonment of impressment was a precondition for any armistice.

2. The Russian Chargé des Affaires at Washington delivered a similar offer of mediation to Madison on March 8, 1813.

3. Samuel Flagg Bemis, *John Quincy Adams and the Foundations of American Foreign Policy* (New York: A. A. Knopf, 1950), 186.

4. Fred L. Engleman, *The Peace of Christmas Eve* (New York: Harcourt, Brace and World, [1962]), 120.

5. Under the regulations of 1808, the flag officers of the Royal Navy were divided into three ranks—admirals, vice admirals, and rear admirals—and each rank was divided into three color-designated squadrons—white, red, and blue. By way of illustration, when Lord Nelson was in command at the Battle of Trafalgar, he held the rank of Vice Admiral of the White.

6. Henry Adams, *History of the United States of America, 1801–1817* 4 vols. (New York: Albert and Charles Boni, 1930) 4:27.

7. Engleman, *The Peace of Christmas Eve,* 251.

8. In its final form, the treaty consisted of eleven articles. (1) Hostilities to cease as soon as both sides ratify the treaty. Except for the Passamaquoddy Islands, everything captured should be restored. (2) The timetable for the cessation of hostilities in various parts of the world. (3) Mutual restoration of prisoners of war and payment in specie of any sums advanced to the prisoners while in captivity. (4) Mutual claims to the Passamaquoddy Islands to be referred to two commissioners, one appointed by each side, who will decide the issue in accordance with "the true intent" of the Treaty of 1783. If the two commissioners can't agree, the matter is to be referred to a friendly sovereign or state. (5) Two commissioners to be appointed, one from each side, to fix the boundary from the source of the St. Croix River to the Iroquois or Cataraguy River, and to particularize the latitude and longitude of the northwest angle of Nova Scotia, the northwesternmost head of the Connecticut River, and such other points of the boundary as they think proper. If the commissioners cannot reach agreement, the matter is to be referred to a friendly sovereign or state. (6) Two commissioners, one from each side, to determine the boundaries along the Iroquois or Cataraguy Rivers and the Great Lakes. In the event of the commissioners failing to agree, the matter is to be referred to a friendly sovereign or state. (7) When the two commissioners have fixed the previous boundary, they are to determine the boundary extending from the water communication between Lake Huron and Lake Superior to the most northwestern point of the Lake of the Woods. They are to determine the ownership of the islands in the lakes, water communications, and rivers forming the boundary, survey and mark the boundary, and particularize the latitude and longitude of the most northwestern point of the Lake of the Woods. In the event of a disagreement, the matter is to be referred to a friendly sovereign or state. (8) The boards of the two commissioners mentioned in the four preceding articles have the power to appoint a secretary and employ surveyors or other persons deemed necessary. They must keep duplicates of their journal, declarations, statements, decisions, and accounts, and deliver them to their respective governments. The commissioners shall be paid in a manner agreed to by both governments. Their expenses will be shared equally by both governments. In the event of the death, resignation, illness, or absence of a commissioner, he is to be replaced in the same manner as the first appointee. If any islands mentioned in the preceding articles change hands as a result of the decisions of the commissioners, all grants of land made previous to the war will be honored. (9) Both sides are to put an end to the hostilities against the Indians and restore to such tribes or nations all the possessions, rights, and privileges they enjoyed in 1811, provided such

Indians agree to cease hostilities. (10) The slave trade is irreconcilable with the principles of humanity and justice, and both sides will continue their best efforts to abolish it. (11) Both parties are to ratify the treaty without change within four months.

9. The sources consulted for this paper are as follows: Samuel F. Bemis, *John Quincy Adams and the Foundations of American Foreign Policy*, vol. 1 (New York: A. A. Knopf, 1950); Fred L. Engleman, *The Peace of Christmas Eve* (New York: Harcourt, Brace and World, [1962]); Raymond Walters, Jr., *Albert Gallatin: Jeffersonian Financier and Diplomat* (New York: Macmillan Publishing Co., 1957); Henry Adams, *History of the United States of America, 1801–1817*, vols. 3–4. (New York: Albert and Charles Boni, 1930); Irving Brant, *James Madison: Commander in Chief, 1812–1836* (Indianapolis: Bobbs, Merrill, 1961); Harry L. Coles, *The War of 1812* (Chicago: University of Chicago Press, 1965); J. Mackay Hitsman, *The Incredible War of 1812: A Military History* (Toronto: University of Toronto Press, 1965); Reginald Horsman, *The War of 1812* (New York: A. A. Knopf, 1969), and *The Diplomacy of the New Republic, 1776–1815* (Arlington Heights, Ill.: Harlan, Davidson, 1985); Samuel Eliot Morison, *Harrison Gray Otis, 1765–1848: The Urbane Federalist* (Boston: Houghton Mifflin, 1969); Bradford Perkins, *Castlereagh and Adams: England and the United States, 1812–1823* (Berkeley: University of California Press, 1964); J. C. A. Stagg, *Mr. Madison's War* (Princeton: Princeton University Press, 1983); and Patrick C. T. White, *A Nation on Trial: America and the War of 1812* (New York: John Wiley & Sons, 1965).

Historiography of the War of 1812

1. Ernest A. Cruikshank, "The Contest for the Command of Lake Erie in 1812–13," in *The Defended Border: Upper Canada and the War of 1812*, ed. Morris Zaslow and Wesley B. Turner (Toronto: Macmillan Publishing Co., 1964), 92.

2. C. P. Stacey, "Another Look at the Battle of Lake Erie," in *Defended Border*, 108–9, 110.

3. James Hannay, *History of the War of 1812 Between Great Britain and the United States of America* (Toronto: Morang, 1905), 184.

4. J. Mackay Hitsman, *The Incredible War of 1812* (Toronto: University of Toronto Press, 1965), 152; Cruikshank, "The Contest," in *Defended Border*, 93–94; Pierre Berton, *Flames Across the Border, 1813–1814* (Toronto: Macmillan Publishing Co., 1981), 133; Hannay, *History of the War*, 187.

5. Stacey, "Another Look," in *Defended Border*, 113; Berton, *Flames Across the Border*, 171.

6. George F. G. Stanley, *The War of 1812: Land Operations* (Toronto: MacMillan of Canada, 1983), 208–9; Hitsman, *The Incredible War*, 156; Berton, *Flames Across the Border*, 182.

7. Alexander Clark Casselman, ed., *Richardson's War of 1812* (Toronto: Historical Publishing, 1902), 212; Katherine B. Coutts, "Thamesville and the Battle of the Thames," in *Defended Border*, 119–20; Stanley, *The War of 1812*, 212; Berton, *Flames Across the Border*, 203.

8. Berton, *Flames Across the Border*, 204; Casselman, *Richardson's War*, 213.

9. Berton, *Flames Across the Border*, 208.

10. Casselman, *Richardson's War*, 222.

11. Stanley, *The War of 1812,* 207; Hitsman, *The Incredible War,* 155; Cruikshank, "The Contest," in *Defended Border,* 103; Coutts, "Thamesville," in *Defended Border,* 118.

12. Hannay, *History of the War,* 200.

13. Victor Lauriston, "The Case for General Procter," in *Defended Border,* 127.

14. S. Antal, "Myths and Facts Concerning General Procter," *Ontario History* 79 (September 1987): 252, 258, 260–61.

15. Berton, *Flames Across the Border,* 207–8.

16. Fred Landon, *Western Ontario and the American Frontier* (Toronto: McClelland and Stewart, 1967), 26, 40; Berton, *Flames Across the Border,* 208.

17. Stanley, *The War of 1812,* 213, 214; Hannay, *History of the War,* 201; Cruikshank, "The Contest," in *Defended Border,* 104; Gerald Craig, *Upper Canada: The Formative Years, 1784–1841* (Toronto: McClelland and Stewart, 1963), 79.

An Aerial View of Put-in-Bay

1. Complete citations for the principal books mentioned in the text are: James Fenimore Cooper, *The Battle of Lake Erie; or, Answers to Messrs. Burges, Duer, and Mackenzie* (Cooperstown: H. & E. Phinney, 1843); Richard H. Dillon, *We Have Met the Enemy: Oliver Hazard Perry, Wilderness Commodore* (New York: McGraw-Hill, 1978); John C. Fredriksen, *Free Trade and Sailors' Rights: A Bibliography of the War of 1812* (Westport: Greenwood Press, 1985); Alexander Slidell Mackenzie, *The Life of Commodore Oliver Hazard Perry* (New York: Harper, 1840); Alfred Thayer Mahan, *Sea Power in Its Relations to the War of 1812,* 2 vols. (Boston: Little, Brown and Company, 1905); *The Naval War of 1812: A Documentary History,* ed. William S. Dudley, et al. (Washington: Naval Historical Center, 1985–); Usher Parsons, *Brief Sketches of the Officers Who Were in the Battle of Lake Erie* (Albany: J. Munsell, 1862); Charles Oscar Paullin, ed., *The Battle of Lake Erie: A Collection of Documents, Chiefly by Commodore Perry* (Cleveland: Rowfant Club, 1918); Max Rosenberg, *The Building of Perry's Fleet on Lake Erie, 1812–1813* (Harrisburg: Pennsylvania Historical and Museum Commission, 1950); J. C. A. Stagg, *Mr. Madison's War: Politics, Diplomacy, and Warfare in the Early American Republic, 1783–1830* (Princeton: Princeton University Press, 1983); William Charles Henry Wood, ed., *Select British Documents of the Canadian War of 1812* (Toronto: Champlain Society, 1920–1928).

2. Mahan, *Sea Power,* 2:99.

3. A new interpretation of Elliott appears in Lawrence J. Friedman and David Curtis Skaggs, "Jesse Duncan Elliott and the Battle of Lake Erie: The Case of Mental Instability," *Journal of the Early Republic* (forthcoming).

4. A special issue of *The Journal of Erie Studies* (vol. 17, no. 2 [fall 1988]), devoted entirely to the Battle of Lake Erie and including important new interpretations by Frederick C. Drake and Michael A. Palmer, appeared simultaneously with the conference at which this paper was originally presented; Seebert J. Goldowsky's *Yankee Surgeon: The Life and Times of Usher Parsons, 1788–1868* (Boston: Francis A. Countway Library of Medicine in cooperation with the Rhode Island Publications Society, 1988) was published a few weeks later.

United States Manuscript Sources for a Study of the War of 1812

1. Reginald Horsman, *The War of 1812* (New York: Alfred A. Knopf, 1969), 273.

2. The complete citations for the works cited by Horsman are: J. Mackay Hitsman, *The Incredible War of 1812: A Military History* (Toronto: University of Toronto Press, 1965); Harry L. Coles, *The War of 1812* (Chicago and London: University of Chicago Press, 1965).

3. John C. Fredriksen, comp., *Resource Guide for the War of 1812* (Los Angeles, Subia, 1979).

4. Pierre Berton, *The Invasion of Canada, 1812–1813* (Boston: Little, Brown and Company, 1980), and *Flames Across the Border: The Canadian-American Tragedy, 1813–1814* (Boston: Little, Brown and Company, 1981).

5. J. C. A. Stagg, *Mr. Madison's War: Politics, Diplomacy, and Warfare in the Early American Republic, 1783–1830* (Princeton: Princeton University Press, 1983).

6. Horsman, *War of 1812,* 272.

Index

Contributors

GERARD T. ALTOFF has served since 1979 as the historian and chief ranger for the National Park Service at Perry's Victory and International Peace Memorial, South Bass Island, Lake Erie. He joined the National Park Service in 1972 after completing four years in the U.S. Coast Guard, including a tour of duty in Vietnam. He worked at Zion National Park and Theodore Roosevelt National Park prior to transferring to his present position.

For the past ten years Altoff has conducted research into the Battle of Lake Erie. The Great Lakes Historical Society recently published his study of the soldiers who volunteered to serve on the American fleet. In 1987 he presented a paper for the "War on the Great Lakes" Symposium at Monroe, Michigan, concerning Oliver Hazard Perry and the Battle of Lake Erie; this paper subsequently appeared in the fall 1989 issue of the *Michigan Historical Review* and was recently printed in booklet form. He contributed two chapters to the Ohio Sea Grant book *The Great Lake Erie,* published in the *Northwest Ohio Quarterly,* and has written numerous articles for newspapers and special interest military periodicals.

DENNIS CARTER-EDWARDS is a research historian with the Ontario Regional Office of Environment Canada, Canadian Parks Service. He is responsible for research requirements for the military sites operated by Parks in Ontario. He has written extensively on military topics dealing with the British Garrisons in Upper Canada, including a structural history of Fort Amherstburg, the 41st and 89th Regiments, military trades, the Commissariat Department, and strategic planning for the defense of Upper Canada during the 1840s. Mr. Carter-Edwards has also contributed to the *Dictionary of Canadian Biography.* He has a personal as well as professional interest in the heritage movement and has written and lectured on local preservation issues.

DOUGLAS E. CLANIN has been an editor at the Indiana Historical Society, Indianapolis, since October 1980. He is currently preparing a microfilm edition of the papers of William Henry Harrison, 1800–1815, which is sponsored by the society. A native of Anderson, Indiana, Clanin graduated from Indiana University-Bloomington (M.A., 1964) and did postgraduate work at the University of Wisconsin-Madison.

At the Indiana Historical Society, Clanin has edited or coedited the following books: John W. Miller, *Indiana Newspaper Bibliography* (1982); James H. Madison, *Indiana through Tradition and Change* (1982); and Edmund F. Ball, annotator, *California Gold Rush: The Diary of Charles H. Harvey, February 12–November 12, 1852* (1983). Clanin was also an assistant editor at the University of Wisconsin-Madison on two multivolume projects edited by the late Merrill Jensen, *The Documentary of the First Federal Elections, 1788–1790,* and *The Documentary History of the Ratification of the Constitution, 1787–1790.*

In addition to presenting papers at meetings of the Indiana Historical Society and the Society for Historians of the Early American Republic, Clanin has published three articles: "Internal Improvements in National Politics, 1816–1830" in *Transportation and the Early Nation* (1982); "A Phoenix Rising from the Ashes: The William Henry Harrison Papers Project" in *Documentary Editing* 10 (June 1988); and "The Correspondence of William Henry Harrison and Oliver Hazard Perry, July 5, 1813–July 13, 1815" in *Northwest Ohio Quarterly* 60 (Autumn 1988).

W. A. B. DOUGLAS was born in Southern Rhodesia (Zimbabwe) in 1929 and was educated in England and Canada. He received his Ph.D. from Queen's University at Kingston, Ontario, in 1973, and served in the Royal Canadian Navy, 1950–73. He specialized in navigation, acted as naval staff officer at the Royal Military College of Canada from 1964 to 1967, and served in the Directorate of History, 1967–73. He became its director when he retired from the Navy.

In 1977 he coauthored, with Brereton Greenhous, *Out of the Shadows: Canada in the Second World War,* and in 1986 published *The Creation of a National Air Force: The Offician History of the RCAF, Volume II.* He has written a wide range of articles on naval and aviation history, including "Canadian Naval Historiography" in *Mariner's Mirror,* November 1984.

Douglas is president of the Canadian Nautical Research Society; director of the Friends of the Canadian War Museum; and a member of the Canadian Defence Quarterly Advisory Board, the Military Affairs Editorial Board, and the "Freshwater" Editorial Advisory Board.

FREDERICK C. DRAKE is a professor of history at Brock University, St. Catharines, Ontario. He was chairman of the department from 1973 to 1976. He was formerly at the University of Wales, Aberystwyth, and in 1969 and 1970 was chairman of that university's Board of American Studies. In the summer of 1987 he was a visiting professor of history at Cornell University. He has been a member of the Canadian Association for American Studies since 1978 and served as its president from 1987 to 1989. He has lectured on the naval war of 1812 at McMaster University for the Hamilton and Scourge Society, and has given several conference papers in the United States and Canada.

Drake is the author of *The Empire of the Seas: A Biography of Rear Admiral Robert Wilson Shufeldt, USN* (1984), which was awarded the 1985 John Lyman prize in United States Naval History by the North American Society for Oceanic History. He has published articles in numerous journals, and has written articles on diplomatic and naval history in *The Encyclopedia of Southern History* and the *Dictionary of Canadian Biography.* He is currently working on *The War of 1812: Naval Operations,* the companion volume to George Stanley's *The War of 1812: Land Operations,* and is also working on a separate, detailed study of the Lakes and River War of 1812 in Canada.

R. DAVID EDMUNDS is professor of history at Indiana University. A specialist in Native American history, he received his Ph.D. in 1972 from the University of Oklahoma. His recent publications include *Tecumseh and the Quest for Indian Leadership* (1984) and *Kinsmen Through Time: An Annoted Bibliography of Potawatomi History* (1987).

In 1978, Dr. Edmunds received the Francis Parkman prize in American History for his work *The Potawatomis: Keepers of the Fire. The Shawnee Prophet* (1983) was nominated for the Pulitzer Prize and was awarded the Ohioana prize for biography in 1984. Dr. Edmunds's other achievements include the Chancellor's Award for Research and Creative Activity (1985) and the Millikin University Alumni Achievement Award (1986).

HAROLD D. LANGLEY is curator of Naval History at the Smithsonian Institution, a position he has held since 1979. He is also an adjunct professor of history at Catholic University of America. His research interests include United States diplomatic and social history and nineteenth-century United States military and naval history. His publications include articles in *Pennsylvania History, Pacific Historical Review,* and *Journal of Negro History.* In 1974 he coedited *Roosevelt and Churchill: Their Secret Wartime Correspondence.*

CHRISTOPHER MCKEE is Samuel R. and Marie-Louise Rosenthal Professor and Librarian of the college at Grinnell College, Grinnell, Iowa. He is the author of *Edward Preble: A Naval Biography, 1761–1807,* and he has contributed chapters on the nineteenth-century United States Navy to *A Guide to the Sources of United States Military History,* edited by Robin Higham and Donald Mrozek. Mr. McKee's recent articles include "The Pathology of a Profession: Death in the United States Navy Officer Corps, 1797–1815" in the May 1985 issue of *War & Society,* awarded the U.S. Naval History Prize for the best article published in 1985, and "Foreign Seamen in the United States Navy: A Census of 1808" in the July 1985 issue of the *William and Mary Quarterly.* His current projects are a social history of the formative years—1794–1815—of the officer corps of the U.S. Navy, to be published in 1991, and a history of naval enlisted men during the nineteenth and early twentieth centuries.

IAN C. B. PEMBERTON was born in Montreal, Quebec, in 1936, and received his Ph.D. in history from the University of Western Ontario in 1973. He joined the faculty of the University of Windsor as a lecturer in 1968, and at present holds the position of associate professor.

Pemberton's basic research interest is Canadian-American relations in the late eighteenth and early nineteenth centuries. His publications include articles in the *Dictionary of Canadian Biography,* the *Loyalist Gazette,* and *Vermont History.* Currently he is working on a study of the political and economic relationship between Canada and Vermont when the latter was an independent republic (1777–91).

STUART SUTHERLAND has been employed since 1974 as a researcher and manuscript editor at the *Dictionary of Canadian Biography;* and in 1980 he became a senior manuscript editor. Mr. Sutherland received his B.A. from Queen's University at Kingston and has contributed biographies to four volumes of the *Dictionary of Canadian Biography.* He has also contributed articles to the *Canadian Encyclopedia,* the *Dictionary of Hamilton Biography,* and modeling and military history magazines. At present Mr. Sutherland is compiling a register of British Army officers during the War of 1812 and is assembling material on the fencible regiments in British North America, 1803 to 1816.

WAR ON THE GREAT LAKES

was composed in 11/12 Bembo on a Varityper system
by Professional Book Compositors, Inc.;
printed by sheet-fed offset on 55-pound Glatfelter B-16 stock,
Smyth sewn and bound over .088″ binders' boards
in Holliston Roxite cloth, with 80-pound Rainbow Antique endleaves,
and wrapped with dust jackets printed in two colors
on 80-pound enamel stock and film laminated;
also adhesive bound with paper covers printed in two colors
on 10′ C1S stock and film laminated
by Cushing-Malloy, Inc.;
designed by Will Underwood;
and published by

THE KENT STATE UNIVERSITY PRESS
Kent, Ohio 44242